Helmut Beißer · Jürgen Büttner

Arbeits-Wortschatz Englisch

Björn Leykauf
Ahornweg 7
91629 Weihenzell

VERLAG SABINE LEONHARDT

Bestellungen ☎ (09131) 2 11 90

FAX 24780

oder über den Buchhandel

ISBN 3-9801773-1-9

3., neubearbeitete Auflage

Druck: Gruner Druck GmbH, Sonnenstraße 23b, 91058 Erlangen

INHALT

Lernen mit dem Arbeitswortschatz

Der "Arbeitswortschatz Englisch" ist ein Lern- und Arbeitsbuch für Fortgeschrittene, die sich mit der Lektüre englischsprachiger Texte beschäftigen, und für Schüler, die sich auf den Abschluss einer weiterführenden Schule vorbereiten und dort mit Textaufgabe und Übersetzung konfrontiert werden. Es ist lehrbuchunabhängig und kann je nach erreichtem Wissensstand unterschiedlich eingesetzt werden: Ziel-setzung

- Schüler und Studierende, die nach beruflicher Tätigkeit wieder die Schule besuchen oder dies zu tun beabsichtigen, können ihren Wortschatz auffrischen bzw. aufbauen und erweitern.
- "Vergessliche" Schüler können beim Eintritt in die Oberstufe den Wortschatz wiederholen und ihre Kenntnisse vertiefen.
- Unterrichtsbegleitend kann wichtiger Wortschatz systematisch eingeübt werden.

Wir verzichten in unserer Wortschatzliste auf absoluten Grundwortschatz (beautiful, begin, bottle usw.) und beschränken uns auf eine überschaubare Zahl von Wörtern (1070 Haupteinträge), die in anspruchsvolleren Texten gehäuft auftreten. Auch bei vollständiger Kenntnis des Auswahlwortschatzes wird der gelegentliche Griff zum Wörterbuch nicht zu vermeiden sein, jedoch sind erfahrungsgemäß bis über 90 Prozent eines schultypischen Sachtextes abgedeckt. Wortschatz auswahl

Um den Lernvorgang zu fördern, haben wir auf eine alphabetische Anordnung oder eine Gliederung in Themenkreise verzichtet; vielmehr soll der Kontrast hinsichtlich Bedeutung und Wortart das Lernen erleichtern. Aufbau

Jeweils auf der linken Seite sind die zu lernenden Vokabeln mit den wesentlichsten deutschen Bedeutungen angeordnet. Insbesondere bei der Übersetzung kann es vorkommen, dass keine der angebotenen deutschen Bedeutungen in den Kontext passt; hier zeigen sich naturgemäß die Grenzen eines zweisprachigen Auswahlwortschatzes. Auf der rechten Seite finden sich Anmerkungen zur richtigen Anwendung, Hinweise auf verwandte Wörter, Fehlermöglichkeiten usw. Die Anmerkungen sind wichtig, brauchen aber nicht im eigentlichen Sinne gelernt zu werden, wenn es auch, je nach Kenntnisstand des Lernenden, nützlich sein kann, einzelne Passagen durch Unterstreichung hervorzuheben.

Zur Vertiefung und Wiederholung - unverzichtbarer Bestandteil des Wortschatzerwerbs - werden deutsch-englische Übungssätze, Vokabelübungen und verschiedene Rätsel angeboten. Sie beziehen sich jeweils auf bestimmte Abschnitte, die vor der Bearbeitung der Weiter-führende Übungen einzelnen Aufgaben wiederholt werden sollten. Wir hoffen, dass die Wortschatzarbeit auf diese Weise gelegentlich sogar Spaß machen wird.

Natürlich sind intensives Lesen, Schreiben und vor allem Sprechen notwendig, um eine Fremdsprache wirklich beherrschen zu lernen. Wir glauben jedoch, dass der "Arbeitswortschatz Englisch" auf dem Weg dorthin eine wesentliche Hilfe sein kann.

Besonders bedanken wollen wir uns an dieser Stelle bei Miss Rebecca Wills, Oxford, die uns bei der Bearbeitung des Manuskripts fachkundig unterstützt hat.

Wir wünschen allen Lesern Durchhaltevermögen und guten Erfolg.

Ansbach, Erlangen im Juni 1986 Helmut Beißer Jürgen Büttner

Vorwort zur zweiten Auflage

Im Verlauf von zwei Jahren haben Lehrkräfte und Schüler verschiedener Schularten in erfreulich großer Zahl den *Arbeitswortschatz* verwendet und intensiv getestet. Die vielfältigen Anregungen aus der Lern- und Unterrichtspraxis, die uns erreichten, haben uns veranlasst, im Rahmen der Neuauflage einige kleinere Änderungen vorzunehmen. So ist etwa häufiger als bisher die Lautschrift (in neuer Form) angegeben, einige verzichtbare Vokabeln wurden aus der Liste entfernt und etwa 80 Neueinträge aufgenommen, die den *Arbeitswortschatz* sinnvoll ergänzen sollen.

Vorwort zur dritten Auflage

Viele neue Rückmeldungen von Lehrern und Schülern haben uns zu einer grundlegenden Überarbeitung des *Arbeitswortschatzes* veranlasst. Es hat sich im Übrigen gezeigt, dass die Beherrschung eines soliden Basiswortschatzes auch und gerade dann unverzichtbar ist, wenn in Prüfungen ein einsprachiges Wörterbuch zur Verfügung steht.

Einige Haupteinträge wurden durch zweckmäßigere ersetzt und die Anmerkungen zum Teil erheblich erweitert. Ein übersichtliches und prägnantes Layout erleichtert den Umgang mit dem *Arbeitswortschatz*. In einem zusätzlichen Kapitel sind nach Sprechabsichten gegliederte Redewendungen aufgelistet, die dem Lernenden helfen sollen, sich im Alltagsgespräch, bei Diskussionen und in mündlichen Prüfungen besser zu behaupten.

Ansbach, Erlangen im September 2002 Helmut Beißer Jürgen Büttner

habit	*Gewohnheit*	[1]
prosperous	*erfolgreich; florierend*	[2]
government ['gʌvənmənt]	*Regierung*	
likely	*wahrscheinlich*	[3]
path	*Pfad; Weg*	
rude	*unhöflich; grob*	
to embarrass	*in Verlegenheit bringen*	[4]
crash	*Unfall; Absturz; Krach*	[5]
in vain	*vergeblich*	
yet	*schon; jedoch*	[6]
not yet	*noch nicht*	[7]
as yet	*bis jetzt*	[8]
to urge [ɜːdʒ]	*drängen; dringend bitten*	[9]
row [rəʊ]	*Reihe*	[10]
criticism	*Kritik; Besprechung*	[11]
seat	*Sitz; Platz*	[12]
to achieve [ə'tʃɪːv]	*erreichen; zustande bringen*	[13]
parcel	*Paket*	[14]
to insist (on)	*bestehen (auf)*	[15]
grave	*Grab*	
to elect	*wählen; erwählen*	[16]
satisfaction	*Befriedigung ; Zufriedenheit*	
cheek [tʃɪːk]	*Backe; Wange*	
tender	*zart; weich; empfindlich*	[17]
barrel	*Fass*	
to develop	*entwickeln; sich entwickeln*	[18]
switch	*Schalter*	[19]
satisfactory (to)	*zufrieden stellend (für)*	
to consult [kən'sʌlt]	*um Rat fragen; konsultieren*	[20]

1 **habit** the habit of smoking, of getting up early etc. * He was in the habit of eating lots of ice-cream *(hatte die Angewohnheit)*

2 **prosperous** a prosperous business etc. SYN: flourishing
successful prosperity

3 **likely** He is likely to come *(er kommt wahrscheinlich)* * He'll come as likely as not *(sehr wahrscheinlich)*

4 **embarrass** She was embarrassed by his silly questions * He was embarrassed by lack of money

5 **crash** car crash, air crash * The hammer fell with a great crash ALSO: crash landing *(Bruchlandung)* * crash-helmet *(Sturzhelm)* * crash course *(Intensivkurs)*

6 **yet** Has she come yet? *(Ist sie schon da?)* SYN: already * They worked hard, yet they failed *(jedoch versagten sie)* SYN: However, but

7 **not yet** She has not come yet / She has not yet come

8 **as yet** The secretary has worked quite well as yet SYN: so far

9 **urge** The salesman urged the customer to buy the dictionary ALSO: He urged the workers on *(trieb sie an)*

10 **row** a row of buildings, books on a shelf etc.; a front-row seat BUT: It's your turn *(du bist an der Reihe)* NOTE: row [raʊ] *(Lärm, Streit)* There was a row in the street.

11 **criticism** He was annoyed by my criticism *(Kritik)* * a criticism of a play in a magazine *(Besprechung)* SYN: review

12 **seat** Take a seat! *(Nimm Platz!)* * Is this seat taken? *(ist dieser Platz besetzt?)* * a seat in parliament BUT: The concert takes place on Sunday *(findet statt)*

13 **achieve** achieve a purpose, an aim etc. * He has never achieved anything in all his life BUT: We missed the train *(erreichten den Zug nicht mehr)*

14 **parcel** NOTE: Trust is part and parcel of a successful business relationship *(ein wesentlicher Teil)*

15 **insist** I insist on his coming in time *(Ich bestehe darauf, dass)* I'll do it if you insist *(wenn du darauf bestehst)* ADJ: insistent (hartnäckig)

16 **elect** He was elected chairman, president etc. *(zum Vorsitzenden etc.* gewählt) BUT: to choose (*wählen, auswählen, sich aussuchen)*

17 **tender** tender age, a tender heart * a tender subject *(ein heikles Thema)* * a tender spot *(verwundbare Stelle)*

18 **develop** develop a film, a plan, bad habits etc. * He developed from a tender child to a robust young man NOUN: development *(Entwicklung)*

19 **switch** VERB: to switch on/off the radio, light etc. *(einschalten / ausschalten)* * She can easily switch from English to French *(wechseln zwischen, umschalten)* BUT: counter *(Post- / Bankschalter)*

20 **consult** to consult a person, book etc. NOUN: consultant *(Berater)* * consultation *(Beratung, Befragung)*

repetition	*Wiederholung* [1]
to continue	*fortsetzen* [2]
wing	*Flügel* [3]
former	*früher (adj.); ehemalig* [4]
the former ... the latter	*der erstere ... der letztere*
bare	*nackt, bloß* [5]
barely	*kaum* [6]
scheme [skɪːm]	*Plan; Entwurf; Schema* [7]
to yield [jɪːld]	*nachgeben; einbringen, abwerfen* [8]
mind	*Geist; Verstand* [9]
once more	*noch einmal* [10]
to negotiate [nɪ'gəʊʃɪˌeɪt]	*verhandeln*
tall [tɔːl]	*groß; hoch* [11]
passage	*Durchgang; Korridor; Textabschnitt* [12]
to inquire [ɪn'kwaɪə]	*sich erkundigen* [13]
inquiry	*Nachforschung; Nachfrage,Erkundigung*
fate	*Schicksal*
chain	*Kette; anketten* [14]
tune	*Melodie; Lied* [15]
to improve [im'pruːv]	*verbessern; sich bessern* [16]
brief	*kurz; flüchtig* [17]
youth [juːθ]	*Jugend; Jugendlicher* [18]
conclusion	*(Schluss)folgerung; Abschluss* [19]
sad	*traurig; schlimm*
arm	*Arm; Armlehne*
arms	*Waffen* [20]
to explain (to)	*erklären* [21]
to scare	*Angst machen, erschrecken* [22]

1 **repetition** ADJ: repetitive *(sich wiederholend)* to repeat

2 **continue** The fine weather continues *(dauert an)* * The road continues *(geht weiter)* * He continued work during lunchtime *(arbeitete weiter)* to go on

3 **wing** the wing of an insect, bird, airplane, a house BUT: grand piano *(Konzertflügel)*

4 **former** the former Prime Minister *(der ehemalige P.M.)* * Mr.Heath, formerly Prime Minister, made a speech *(Mr.Heath, der früher Premierminister gewesen war)* * customs of former days *(von früher)* BUT: She used to be rich *(früher war sie reich)*

5 **bare** bare hands; a mountain bare of trees *(ohne Bäume)* ALSO: barefoot (barfuß) naked

6 **barely** I barely know him *(Ich kenne ihn kaum)* SYN: hardly, scarcely

7 **scheme** scheme of work *(Arbeitsplan)* * town development scheme *(Stadtentwicklungsplan)*

8 **yield** The investment yields 10 per cent *(wirft ab)* * He yielded to temptation *(gab der Versuchung nach)*

9 **mind** keep in mind *(merken)*; to change one's mind *(seine Meinung ändern)*; have in mind *(im Sinn haben)*; nothing was further from my mind *(nichts lag mir ferner)* * absent-minded *(geistesabwesend)*

10 **once more** SYN: once again

11 **tall** a tall woman, a tall tower BUT: high heels, high mountains

12 **passage** The police had to force their passage through the people standing outside * He was waiting in the passage * Read that passage again ALSO: She booked her passage to Dover *(Überfahrt)*

13 **inquire** inquire about the way, after a good hotel, after someone's health, for a certain article, into a matter *(nachforschen)*

14 **chain** a chain for dogs, of mountains, of ideas etc * chain reaction VERB: to chain up *(anketten)*

15 **tune** They danced to the tune of 'Yesterday' * The piano is out of tune *(verstimmt)* VERB: tune up an instrument *(stimmen)*, a motor *(einstellen)*

16 **improve** I improved my situation *(verbesserte meine Lage)* * His health gradually improved *(besserte sich allmählich)*

17 **brief** a brief moment, meeting, letter, speech etc.

18 **youth** He was attacked by a gang of youths * I am disappointed of today's youth * In her youth she used to be a good violinist

19 **conclusion** the conclusion of a letter * he came to the conclusion *(Schlussfolgerung)* * the conclusion of a treaty *(Vertragsabschluss)*

20 **arms** The soldiers had plenty of arms *(eine Menge Waffen)* BUT: She could not defend herself as she didn't have any weapon *(keine Waffe)* NOTE: armament / disarmament *(Rüstung / Abrüstung)*

21 **explain** The teacher explained the problem to her students * That explains his behaviour NOUN: explanation

22 **to scare** He is rather scared of dogs SYN: to frighten NOUN: bomb scare *(Bombendrohung)* * It gave me a scare *(machte mir Angst)*

hostile	*feindlich, feindselig*	[1]
to prosper	*gedeihen*	[2]
to govern ['gʌvn]	*regieren*	[3]
to handle	*handhaben; anfassen; behandeln*	[4]
loss	*Verlust*	[5]
to guard (against, from)	*bewachen; schützen (vor)*	[6]
needle [nɪːdl]	*Nadel*	[7]
to gleam	*strahlen; schimmern*	[8]
distribution [dɪstrɪ'bjuːʃən]	*Verteilung*	[9]
to row [rəʊ]	*rudern*	[10]
legislation [ˌledʒɪs'leɪʃn]	*Gesetzgebung*	
embarrassing	*peinlich; unangenehm* SYN unpleasant	
gifted, talented, able	*begabt*	[11]
to recover	*sich erholen; wieder erlangen*	[12]
sacrifice ['sækrɪfaɪs]	*Opfer; opfern*	[13]
to argue ['ɑːgjuː] quarrel	*streiten; argumentieren*	[14]
empty	*leer; leeren*	[15]
to crash	*krachen; zerschmettern*	
urgent ['ɜːdʒənt]	*dringend*	[16]
tin	*Zinn; Konservenbüchse*	
despite / in spite of	*trotz*	
to enjoy	*genießen*, gefallen	[17]
task	*Aufgabe*	[18]
bench [bentʃ]	*Sitzbank*	
envelope	*(Brief)umschlag; Hülle*	
to weigh [weɪ]	*wiegen; abwägen*	
to fit	*passen*	[19]
to remain	*(bestehen) bleiben*	[20]
innocent	*unschuldig* op: guilty	[21]
to burgle (a house)	einbrechen in	

1 **hostile** They were rather hostile to (towards) the newcomers * A desert is a hostile environment NOUN: hostility

2 **prosper** a child, a business etc. prospers NOUN: prosperity *(Gedeihen, Wohlstand)*

3 **govern** to govern a city, a country ALSO: He governed his rage *(zügelte seine Wut)* * She was governed by the idea of becoming a famous actress one day *(von der Vorstellung beherrscht)*

4 **handle** handle a situation, people, books etc. NOUN: the handle of a cup, suitcase etc. *(Griff)* to deal with/un

5 **loss** NOTE: He was at a loss for words *(um Worte verlegen / wusste nicht, was er sagen sollte)*

6 **guard** The prisoners were guarded by soldiers *(bewacht)* * Warm clothes guarded them against the cold *(schützten sie vor der Kälte)* NOUN: the changing of the guard *(Wachablösung)* protect

7 **needle** sewing needle *(Nähnadel)* NOTE: to look for a needle in a haystack BUT: pin *(Stecknadel)*

8 **gleam** NOUN: a gleam of hope *(Hoffnungsschimmer)* * the first gleams of the sun *(die ersten Sonnenstrahlen)* to beam tray

9 **distribution** the distribution of wealth, profit, prizes etc. * plants with a wide distribution *(Verbreitung)* to distribute

10 **row** NOTE: row boat / rowing boat *(Ruderboot)*

11 **gifted** a gifted child, artist etc. BUT: poisoned *(vergiftet)*

12 **recover** recover from illness; recover sight, strength etc. * I hope he will recover soon NOUN: he was glad about the recovery of his keys *(froh, daß er die Schlüssel wiederfand / zurückbekam)*

13 **sacrifice** NOUN: She sold her car at a sacrifice *(mit Verlust)* * to make a sacrifice *(ein Opfer bringen)* BUT: the victim of a murder *(Mordopfer)*

14 **argue** Why must you always be arguing *(immer streiten)* * He argued against the plan *(argumentierte gegen)* NOUN: They had endless arguments *(endlose Streitereien)* * a good argument *(Argument)*

15 **empty** an empty room, plate, promise, threat etc. NOUN: emptiness *(die Leere)*

16 **urgent** an urgent message, order, need etc. * I urgently wanted to see her

17 **enjoy** enjoy a theatre performance, a meal, a high income etc. * She enjoys rowing the boat across the lake.

18 **task** NOTE: to set someone a task *(jemandem eine Aufgabe stellen)* * task force *(Sondereinheit der Polizei oder des Militärs)*

19 **fit** That dress fits! ADJ: He wasn't fit for the job *(geeignet)*

20 **remain** They remained at home * This remains to be seen ALSO: Not a bit remained of the Christmas pudding *(blieb übrig)*

21 **innocent** He was innocent of the crime NOUN: innocence

to belong to		*gehören; gehören zu*	[1]
authority	[ɔːˈθɒretɪ]	*Autorität; Behörde; (Befehls)gewalt; (Macht)befugnis*	[2]
critic		*Kritiker; Kunstkenner*	
urgency	[ˈɜːdʒənsɪ]	*Dringlichkeit*	[3]
to dismiss		*entlassen*	[4]
guilty	[ˈgɪltɪ]	*schuldig*	[5]
to happen		*sich ereignen; geschehen*	[6]
moreover	[mɔːˈrəʊvə]	*überdies; außerdem*	[7]
commerce	[ˈkɒmɜːs]	*Handel*	[8]
stock		*Lager; Vorrat*	[9]
stocks		*Aktien*	
unless	[ənˈles]	*wenn nicht, falls nicht, außer*	[10]
wise	[waɪz]	*weise, klug*	[11]
wisdom	[ˈwɪzdəm]	*Weisheit, Klugheit*	
stomach	[ˈstʌmək]	*Magen*	
remedy (for)		*Mittel (gegen)*	[12]
puzzle		*Rätsel; vor ein Rätsel stellen*	[13]
to replace		*ersetzen*	[14]
whole		*ganz*	[15]
on the whole		*im Großen und Ganzen*	
to rob		*(be)rauben*	[16]
thorough	[ˈθʌrə]	*gründlich*	[17]
whistle	[wɪsl]	*pfeifen; (Triller)pfeife*	
to satisfy		*befriedigen, zufriedenstellen*	
election		*Wahl (durch Stimmabgabe)*	
to repeat		*wiederholen*	[18]
official		*offiziell; Beamter*	
twice		*zweimal*	[19]
ultimate	[ˈʌltɪmət]	*äußerst; entferntest; endgültig*	[20]

1 **belong to** NOUN: The thieves stole all my belongings *(meine ganze Habe)* to own / owner

2 **authority** A teacher is a person of authority * She is one of the leading authorities on stomach diseases * Only the police have the authority to arrest people * local authorities *(örtliche Behörden)* VERB: to authorize *(ermächtigen)*

3 **urgency** a matter of great urgency *(eine sehr dringende Angelegenheit)*

4 **dismiss** He dismissed the maid for bad behaviour *(wegen schlechten Benehmens)* * The teacher dismisses her class after the lesson *(lässt sie gehen)* * As the water was rather cold we dismissed the idea of having a swim *(gaben das Vorhaben auf)*

5 **guilty** NOUN: Their guilt remained doubtful *(blieb zweifelhaft)*

6 **happen** The accident happened late at night ALSO: I happen to know her *(Ich kenne sie zufällig)*

7 **moreover** I like this pub, moreover it's quite near SYN: in addition, besides

8 **commerce** The commerce between the two countries developed well NOTE: chamber of commerce *(Handelskammer)*

9 **stock** Sorry, the book is out of stock *(nicht auf Lager)* * stock-exchange *(Börse)* VERB: He stocked all sorts of pipes *(führte)* BUT: stick *(der Stock)*

10 **unless** I'll go there unless it rains

11 **wise** NOTE: He came from the meeting none the wiser *(genauso klug wie zuvor)*

12 **remedy** There is no remedy for old age * The patient was beyond remedy *(Dem Patienten konnte nicht mehr geholfen werden)*

13 **puzzle** VERB: He puzzled his brain *(zerbrach sich den Kopf)* * I was puzzled by his reaction *(verblüfft)* ALSO: riddle *(Rätsel, Rätselfrage)*

14 **replace** The motor had to be replaced by a new one *(musste ersetzt werden)* ALSO: Please replace that vase *(stelle sie zurück)*

15 **whole** a whole cup *(ganz, nicht zerbrochen)* * the whole cake, a whole hour, your whole energy, the whole of my money BUT: hole *(Loch)*

16 **rob** The bank was robbed *(wurde ausgeraubt)* * I was robbed of my coat *(Mein Mantel wurde mir gestohlen)* NOUN: robbery

17 **thorough** thorough cleaning, instruction; a thorough worker * They searched the arrested man thoroughly *(durchsuchten ihn gründlich)* BUT: through *(durch)*

18 **repeat** ADV: repeatedly *(wiederholt, zum wiederholten Mal)*

19 **twice** once, twice, three times, four times, etc. NOTE: twice as much *(zweimal so viel)*, twice as many *(zweimal so viele)*

20 **ultimate** the ultimate aim, truth, solution etc. * the ultimate destination of a journey ADV: ultimately *(schließlich, im Grunde)*

to interrupt	*unterbrechen*
peculiar [pɪkju:lɪə]	*sonderbar; besonder (er/e/es)* [1]
to collect	*(ein)sammeln* [2]
to approach	*sich nähern* [3]
straw [strɔ:]	*Stroh; Strohhalm* [4]
to conceal (from)	*verbergen (vor)* [5]
in accordance with	*gemäß; in Übereinstimmung mit* [6]
to report (to s.o.)	*(jemd.) berichten* [7]
option	*Möglichkeit; Option*
to mind	*beachten; sich kümmern um* [8]
yield	*Ertrag* [9]
rent	*Miete; Pacht; (ver)mieten* [10]
improvement	*(Ver)besserung; Fortschritt*
necessity	*Notwendigkeit; Bedürfnis* [11]
suburb [ˈsʌbɜ:b]	*Vorstadt; Vorort*
wooden	*hölzern*
tip	*Tip; Spitze; Trinkgeld* [12]
act	*Tat; Gesetz* [13]
servant	*Diener; Dienstmädchen*
civil servant	*Beamter; Beamtin*
till / until	*bis (zu)* [14]
similarity	*Ähnlichkeit*
to abandon	*aufgeben; preisgeben* [15]
raw [rɔ:]	*roh; rauh* [16]
to withdraw	*(sich) zurückziehen* [17]
particular	*besondere(r, s); Einzelheit* [18]
fatal [ˈfeɪtl]	*verhängnisvoll; tödlich* [19]
to deliver	*(aus-/ab-) liefern* [20]
aid	*Hilfe* [21]

1 **peculiar** a peculiar dress *(sonderbar)* * peculiarly interesting *(besonders)* ALSO: a custom peculiar to Red Indians *(ein Brauch, der Indianern eigen ist)*

2 **collect** to collect stamps, money, ideas, one's thoughts ALSO: The mother collected her little son from the kindergarten *(holte ihn ab)*

3 **approach** They approached the problem *(näherten sich dem Problem)* * Summer is approaching (*Es wird Sommer*) * They approached him about some money (*wandten sich an ihn*)

4 **straw** NOTE: man of straw *(Strohmann)* * the last straw that breaks the camel's neck *(der Tropfen, der das Fass zum Überlaufen bringt)*

5 **conceal** SYN: hide NOTE: hiding-place *(Versteck)*

6 **accordance** He acted in accordance with the regulations *(handelte gemäß den Bestimmungen)*

7 **report** NOTE: school report *(Zeugnis)*

8 **mind** to mind a child, a shop etc. ALSO: Mind the step *(Vorsicht Stufe!)* * Mind the dog *(Warnung vor dem Hund)* * Do you mind my smoking? *(Macht es Ihnen etwas aus, wenn ich rauche?)*

9 **yield** the farmer's yield of grain *(Getreideertrag)* * the yield on his shares *(Dividende auf seine Aktien)*

10 **rent** house for rent *(zu vermieten)* * a rentable house *(Haus, das man mieten kann)* BUT: a profitable business *(ein rentables Geschäft)* * an old age pension *(Rente)*

11 **necessity** Food is a necessity of life *(Grundbedürfnis)* ALSO: a case of necessity *(Notfall)*

12 **tip** Be wise and take my tip SYN: advice * a finger-tip, the tip of an iceberg * It's the custom to give the waiter a tip

13 **act** The Clean Air Act of 1956 *(Gesetz zur Reinhaltung der Luft)* ALSO: the fifth act of Hamlet *(Akt)* VERB: to act *(handeln)*

14 **till** conjunction: We have to stay till he comes *(warten, bis er kommt)* * preposition: They worked till midday *(bis Mittag;)* * We don't expect him till five *(nicht vor fünf)*

15 **abandon** Due to the enormous problems they had to abandon their plan * The damaged ship had to be abandoned

16 **raw** raw material, raw meat, raw winds etc.

17 **withdraw** They withdrew their support * After the first attack the enemy withdrew ALSO: to withdraw money from a bank account *(Geld abheben)*

18 **particular** He did it for no particular reason *(aus keinem besonderen Grund)* * Please go into particulars *(gib Einzelheiten)*

19 **fatal** The affair was fatal to the politician's career * a fatal accident

20 **deliver** The mail is delivered every day ALSO: He delivered a speech *(hielt eine Rede)* NOUN: delivery *(Lieferung)*

21 **aid** They came immediately to their aid NOTE: first aid *(erste Hilfe)* * foreign aid *(Entwicklungshilfe)* * hearing aid *(Hörgerät)*

particularly/in particular	*besonders, insbesondere*	[1]
to regret	*bedauern*	[2]
else	*sonst (noch), anders*	[3]
awkward ['ɔːkwəd]	*schwierig, ungünstig; unbeholfen*	[4]
consent [kən'sent]	*Zustimmung, Einwilligung*	[5]
to declare	*erklären; verkünden*	[6]
wreck [rek]	*Wrack; Schiffbruch; zugrunde richten*	
target	*Ziel*	[7]
to bury ['berɪ]	*begraben; vergraben*	[8]
up to	*bis zu*	[9]
eventually	*schließlich, endlich*	[10]
to cause	*verursachen*	[11]
handsome	*gut aussehend; stattlich*	[12]
to announce	*ankündigen; ansagen; bekanntgeben*	
stuff	*Zeug*	[13]
considerable	*beträchtlich; bedeutend*	[14]
mail	*Post*	[15]
achievement [ə'tʃiːvmənt]	*Leistung; Ausführung*	[16]
luck	*Glück*	[17]
meanwhile / meantime	*mittlerweile. inzwischen*	
happiness	*Zufriedenheit; Glück*	
to annoy	*verärgern; belästigen*	[18]
loose	*lose, locker*	[19]
population	*Bevölkerung*	
annual ['ænjuəl]	*jährlich*	[20]
relation	*Beziehung; Verwandte(r)*	[21]
to omit	*auslassen*	
focus	*Brennpunkt; Zentrum*	[22]

1 **particularly** I remembered her in particular *(erinnerte mich besonders an sie)* SYN: especially

2 **regret** NOUN: To my regret I can't come *(zu meinem Bedauern)*

3 **else** Did you notice anything else? *(sonst noch etwas?)* * ask someone else *(jemand anderen)* * Thank you, nothing else *(nichts mehr)* ALSO: You must come, or else she'll be angry SYN: otherwise

4 **awkward** After we had lost our way things became very awkward * 7 o'clock is a very awkward time for me * He felt a bit awkward in his new class *(unbeholfen, unsicher)*

5 **consent** They married without the consent of their parents VERB: to consent *(einwilligen)*

6 **declare** ALSO: Have you anything to declare? *(Haben Sie etwas zu verzollen?)*

7 **target** the target of criticism, of an attack, a target for shooting, a sales target NOTE: to meet a target *(ein Ziel erreichen)*

8 **bury** The dog buried its bone * He buried himself in his books She sat there buried in thought *(gedankenverloren)*

9 **up to** She counted up to ten *(bis zehn)* NOTE: What is he up to? *(was hat er vor?)* * He is up to no good *(führt etwas im Schilde)* * Up to now they haven't lost a single game

10 **eventually** SYN: finally BUT: possibly, perhaps *(eventuell)*

11 **cause** The death of the trees was caused by acid rain *(wurde vom sauren Regen verursacht)* * The heavy rain caused the water to rise *(ließ es ansteigen)*

12 **handsome** a handsome man, horse, building, profit, gift etc.

13 **stuff** NOTE: food stuffs *(Lebensmittel)* * Stuff and nonsense! *(So ein Schwachsinn!)* * She's of the right stuff *(aus dem richtigen Holz geschnitzt)*

14 **considerable** a considerable price, distance, weight etc. ALSO: a considerable man *(ein bedeutender Mann)*

15 **mail** There is a lot of mail today NOTE: air mail *(Luftpost)* * mailbox SYN: letter-box *(Briefkasten)* * mail-man SYN: postman BUT: post-office *(Postamt)*

16 **achievement** The landing on the moon was a great achievement of space technology * The plan was simple but its achievement turned out to be rather difficult

17 **luck** good / bad luck (Glück / Pech) ADJ: She was lucky to find her keys again *(hatte Glück)* * a lucky shot *(Glückstreffer)* BUT: a happy marriage *(glückliche Ehe)*

18 **annoy** I was very annoyed with her *(ärgerte mich sehr über sie)* * They were annoyed at the delay *(verärgert über die Verspätung)* Some annoyances didn't spoil our holidays *(Ärgernisse)*

19 **loose** The screw worked loose *(die Schraube lockerte sich)* * She has a loose tongue *(ein loses Mundwerk)* BUT: to lose *(verlieren)*

20 **annual** They developed a new programme at their annual meeting * The meeting takes place annually *(einmal im Jahr)*

21 **relation** relation between parents and children; business relation *(Geschäftsbeziehung)* * All his relations came to his birthday party

22 **focus** He is always the focus of attention VERB: All eyes were focused on her *(richteten sich auf sie)*

modest ['mɒdɪst]	*bescheiden* [1]
to persuade [pə'sweɪd]	*überzeugen; überreden* [2]
laughter ['lɑːftə]	*Gelächter* [3]
filthy	*schmutzig; scheußlich* [4]
genuine ['dʒenjuɪn]	*echt* [5]
to move	*bewegen* [6]
movement / move	*Bewegung* [7]
necessary (necessity)	*notwendig, nötig*
admiration	*Bewunderung* [8]
to take down	*herunternehmen; aufschreiben* [9]
to take for	*halten für* [10]
to take off (SYN: touch-down)	*weg-/abnehmen; ausziehen(Kleidung); starten (Flugzeug)* [11]
to take to	*die Gewohnheit annehmen* [12]
quiet	*ruhig, still; Ruhe* [13]
to preach [priːtʃ]	*predigen* [14]
single	*einzeln; einzig; Unverheiratete(r)* [15]
to unite [juː'naɪt]	*(sich) vereinigen* [16]
union	*Gewerkschaft; Union* [17]
collar	*Kragen; Halsband*
white-collar work/worker	*Büroarbeit / -angestellter*
blue-collar worker	*Arbeiter(in)*
association	*Vereinigung; Gesellschaft; Verband*
stop	*Haltestelle; Aufenthalt; Pause; aufhören; anhalten* [18]
courage ['kʌrɪdʒ]	*Mut* [19]
significant	*bezeichnend; wichtig* [20]
to reject [rɪ'dʒekt]	*ablehnen; zurückweisen* [21]
sensible	*vernünftig* [22]

1 **modest** a modest person, behaviour, house, price, question etc. NOUN modesty *(Bescheidenheit)*

2 **persuade** I could persuade him of my honesty *(Ich konnte ihn von meiner Ehrlichkeit überzeugen)* * Don't try to persuade me to do such things *(versuche nicht, mich dazu zu überreden)*

3 **laughter** NOTE: to burst into laughter *(in Gelächter ausbrechen)*

4 **filthy** ALSO: He likes telling filthy jokes NOUN: filth *(Schmutz, Dreck)*

5 **genuine** genuine leather, pearls, sorrows, concerns etc.

6 **movement** the civil rights movement * The lion didn't make any movement **move** What will be your next move? *(dein nächster Schritt)* * She made a move towards him *(bewegte sich auf ihn zu)* He never sits still; he is always on the move *(immer in Bewegung)*

7 **move** ALSO: They were moving house *(zogen um)* * move in /out ein-/ausziehen) * We were moved to tears *(zu Tränen gerührt)*

8 **admiration** We were filled with admiration *(voller Bewunderung)*

9 **take down** Take down those books from the shelf *(nimm herunter)* Please take down notes *(machen Sie Notizen)*

10 **take for** I took him for a thief *(hielt ihn für einen Dieb)* * to take something for granted *(etwas als selbstverständlich ansehen)*

11 **take off** take off a beard, a hat, clothes etc. NOUN: ready for take-off *(klar zum Start)*

12 **take to** He took to drink *(wandte sioh dem Alkohol zu)*

13 **quiet** a quiet life, evening, man etc. ALSO: They kept it quiet *(hielten es geheim)*

14 **preach** The vicar preached about charity * Don't preach to me about what I should do NOUN: preacher *(Prediger)* NOTE: sermon *(Predigt)*

15 **single** She did the job in a single day * He didn't say a single word ALSO: She enjoyed being a single *(genoss es, nicht verheiratet zu sein)* * a single-minded person *(zielstrebig)*

16 **unite** They united in fighting the enemy *(vereinigten sich)* * a united effort *(gemeinsame Anstrengung)*

17 **union** the Trade Union Congress *(Gewerkschaftskongress)* * They lived in perfect union *(in vollständiger Einigkeit)*

18 **stop** He stopped smoking *(hörte auf zu rauchen)* * We stopped to have a rest *(hörten auf / hielten an, um uns auszuruhen)* ALSO: stop short *(plötzlich anhalten)* * stop at nothing *(vor nichts zurückschrecken)*

19 **courage** to lose courage *(den Mut verlieren)* * to take up courage *(Mut schöpfen)*

20 **significant** a significant gesture, study, report, improvement NOUN: significance *(Bedeutung, Wichtigkeit)*

21 **reject** The boss rejected my proposal * He often feels rejected NOUN: rejection [rɪ'dʒekʃn]

22 **sensible** a sensible person, plan, decision etc. SYN: reasonable BUT: sensitive *(sensibel)*

to obtain		*erhalten, erlangen*	[1]
purchase	['pɜːtʃəs]	*Anschaffung; Kauf*	[2]
request		*Bitte; Gesuch*	[3]
to be requested		*gebeten, ersucht werden*	[4]
similar		*ähnlich*	
customer	['kʌstəmə]	*Kunde*	
to grade		*abstufen; einteilen*	[5]
declaration		*Erklärung*	[6]
to contemplate		*betrachten; nachdenken*	[7]
thief (pl. thieves)		*Dieb*	
to stuff		*(voll)stopfen*	[8]
announcement		*Ansage; Durchsage; Bekanntgabe*	[9]
to repair		*ausbessern; instandsetzen*	
kind		*freundlich*	[10]
all kinds of		*alle möglichen*	[11]
to laugh (at)	[lɑːf]	*lachen (über)*	
persuasive	[pə'sweɪsɪv]	*überzeugend; redegewandt*	
key	[kɪː]	*Schlüssel; Taste*	[12]
comb	[kəʊm]	*Kamm; kämmen; durchkämmen*	
adequate	['ædɪkwɪt]	*angemessen, adäquat*	[13]
to shelter		*beschirmen; (be)schützen*	[14]
contrary		*entgegengesetzt, gegenteilig*	[15]
message		*Nachricht; Botschaft*	[16]
deep		*tief; unergründlich, dunkel*	[17]
depth		*Tiefe*	[18]
to blame s.o.		*jemandem die Schuld geben*	[19]
pace		*Schritt; Tempo*	[20]
speech		*Rede; Sprache*	[21]
nasty		*scheußlich; unangenehm*	[22]

1 **obtain** We obtained permission to go * They had to wait long but at last they obtained help * Where can I obtain the spare part?

2 **purchase** VERB: to purchase *(anschaffen, erwerben, kaufen)*

3 **request** More information will be given on request *(auf Anfrage)* I've come here at the request of my parents *(auf Bitten)*

4 **be requested** Visitors are requested not to smoke here

5 **grade** graded exercises *(Übungen mit unterschiedl. Schwierigkeitsgrad)* * The parcels were graded by size *(der Größe nach geordnet)* NOUN: a grade in the army *(Rang)* * a high grade of intelligence *(hoher Intelligenzgrad)*

6 **declaration** a declaration of income, war etc. * the Declaration of Independence *(amerikanische Unabhängigkeitserklärung)* BUT: explanation *(Erklärung von Zusammenhängen)*

7 **contemplate** He sat there contemplating the map *(saß da und betrachtete)* * They contemplate moving in next door *(sie erwägen)* NOUN: He stood in contemplation *(stand nachdenklich da)*

8 **stuff** The fat man stuffed himself with food * The candidate was stuffed with facts

9 **announcement** a broadcast announcement; an announcement of death

10 **kind** a kind person, action, etc. * That's very kind of you

11 **kinds of** In the supermarket you can buy all kinds of food stuff

12 **key** The key doesn't fit the lock *(passt nicht zum Schloss)* * He couldn't find the key to the problem

13 **adequate** His income was adequate to his position * They took adequate measures to deal with the situation

14 **shelter** to shelter a plant from wind NOUN: bus shelter *(Wartehäuschen)* * She took shelter from the thunderstorm *(suchte Schutz vor dem Gewitter)*

15 **contrary** He did it contrary to my advice *(gegen meinen Rat)* NOUN: on the contrary *(im Gegenteil)* BUT: in contrast to *(im Gegensatz zu)*

16 **message** He gave me a message * He understood the message of the book

17 **deep** a deep lake, wound, disorder, forest, sleep etc.

18 **depth** She studied Chinese literature in depth *(gründlich)* SYN: thoroughly * When they talk about biochemistry I am out of my depth *(komme ich nicht mehr mit)*

19 **blame** She blamed her brother for the failure * He was not to blame for the accident *(hatte keine Schuld daran)*

20 **pace** eight paces away *(acht Schritte weit weg)* * a slow pace *(geringes Tempo)*, a good pace *(stattliches Tempo)* * They worked at a slow pace *(arbeiteten ziemlich langsam)*

21 **speech** He made / gave a speech *(hielt eine Rede)* * I can tell from your speech where you come from

22 **nasty** nasty weather; a nasty person, smell, accident etc.

ease	*Leichtigkeit; Ruhe; Behaglichkeit*	[1]
persuasion [pə'sweɪʒn]	*Überredung; Überzeugung(skraft)*	[2]
voluntary	*freiwillig*	[3]
to accomplish	*vollenden; ausführen*	[4]
margin ['mɑ:dʒɪn]	*Rand; Spielraum*	[5]
state	*Zustand; Staat*	[6]
rush	*Eile; Andrang*	[7]
operation	*Operation; Arbeitsgang; Verfahren*	[8]
tube [tju:b]	*Rohr; Schlauch; U-Bahn*	[9]
filth	*Schmutz; Verkommenheit*	
to employ	*beschäftigen; verwenden*	[10]
unemployed	*arbeitslos; Arbeitsloser*	
employee [ˌemplɔɪ'ɪ]	*Arbeitnehmer (in)*	
employer [ɪm'plɔɪə]	*Arbeitgeber; Unternehmer*	
debt [det]	*Schuld; Verpflichtung*	[11]
benefit	*Vorteil; Nutzen*	[12]
to escape (from)	*entfliehen; entkommen; entgehen*	[13]
office	*Büro; Amt; Dienst*	
officer	*Beamter; Offizier*	
story	*Geschichte; Erzählung*	[14]
to turn	*drehen; (um)wenden*	[15]
to turn out	*hinauswerfen; produzieren*	[16]
to turn out to be	*sich erweisen als*	[17]
capacity	*Aufnahmefähigkeit; Inhalt*	[18]
gadget ['gædʒɪt]	*Vorrichtung; Apparat*	
to communicate	*mitteilen; übertragen*	[19]
temporary	*zeitweilig; vorübergehend*	[20]
campaign [kæm'peɪn]	*(Werbe)feldzug*	
to apologize	*sich entschuldigen (bei)*	[21]

1 **ease** He solved the task with ease *(mit Leichtigkeit)* * He lived a life of ease *(bequemes Leben)* VERB: The doctor eased him of his pain *(befreite ihn von seinen Schmerzen)*

2 **persuasion** the power of persuasion *(Überredungskunst)* * religious persuasion *(religiöse Überzeugung)* * It is my persuasion that we should give up

3 **voluntary** OPP: involuntary *(unfreiwillig)* NOUN: volunteer *(Freiwilliger)*

4 **accomplish** I was quite surprised to see how much she had accomplished in such a short time

5 **margin** the margin of a book * He caught the train at a comfortable margin *(erreichte ihn ganz bequem)*

6 **state** state of health *(Gesundheitszustand)* * state of the nation *(Lage der Nation)* NOTE: the States *(die Vereinigten Staaten)*

7 **rush** rush hour *(Hauptverkehrszeit)* * He was in a rush *(in Eile)*

8 **operation** ALSO: the machine is in/out of operation *(in/außer Betrieb)*

9 **tube** ALSO: a tube of toothpaste *(Tube Zahnpasta)*; tubeless tyre *(schlauchloser Reifen)*

10 **employ** He employs eleven workers * She employs her spare time wisely

11 **debt** He is in / out of debt (*verschuldet / schuldenfrei)* NOTE: to run into debt *(in Schulden geraten)* BUT: That's your fault *(Das ist deine Schuld)*

12 **benefit** It is to your own benefit if you go now * The advice you gave me wasn't of any benefit to me. ALSO: unemployment benefit, sickness benefit etc. *(Arbeitslosengeld, Krankengeld usw.)*

13 **escape** a prisoner, a bird escapes * you escape punishment, observation etc. * His name escapes me *(fällt mir nicht ein)*

14 **story** NOTE: storey *(Stockwerk)*; American: story * He lives on the second storey

15 **turn** NOTE: turn s.th. upside down *(etwas auf den Kopf stellen)*

16 **turn out** He was turned out of his job (*hinausgeworfen)* * The factory is turning out large quantities of windows *(produziert)*

17 **turn out to be** He turned out to be the winner *(erwies sich als der Gewinner)*

18 **capacity** The lorry has a capacity of five tons * The stadium was filled to capacity * He has a rather limited capacity for new ideas

19 **communicate** communicate information, feelings etc. to someone * They communicated with one another by telephone *(sie unterhielten sich per Telefon)* * There are parents who can't communicate with their children *(sich verständigen)*

20 **temporary** his temporary absence ADV: He was temporarily absent

21 **apologize** He apologized for his bad behaviour BUT: to excuse someone *(jemanden entschuldigen)* * Please excuse my being late

supply and demand		*Angebot und Nachfrage*	
to note		*bemerken, beachten*	[1]
note		*Anmerkung; Notiz*	[2]
once	[wʌns]	*einmal (adv); sobald (conj)*	[3]
once in a while		*hin und wieder*	[4]
at once		*sofort*	[5]
major		*Haupt-; bedeutend*	[6]
strong		*stark, kräftig*	
original		*ursprünglich; Original*	[7]
provided (that)		*vorausgesetzt (dass)*	
staff	[stɑːf]	*Stab; Personal, Belegschaft*	[8]
to compel	[kəmˈpel]	*zwingen*	[9]
to bore		*langweilen*	[10]
safe (from)		*sicher (vor); Geldschrank*	[11]
environment		*Umwelt; Umgebung; Milieu*	
intention		*Absicht; Zweck*	[12]
healthy	[ˈhelθɪ]	*gesund*	[13]
prediction		*Vorhersage*	[14]
offence		*Beleidigung; Vergehen*	[15]
neck		*Hals; Genick*	[16]
seed		*Same (n); Saat*	
tie	[taɪ]	*Verbindung, Beziehung; binden*	[17]
to wrap	[ræp]	*einwickeln; einpacken*	[18]
to succeed (in)		*Erfolg haben (bei)*	[19]
issue	[ˈɪʃuː]	*Angelegenheit; Problem; Ausgabe*	[20]
indication		*Anzeichen; Hinweis*	
to appreciate	[əˈprɪːʃieɪt]	*(hoch) schätzen; (gut) verstehen, anerkennen*	[21]
to contain		*enthalten*	

1 **to note** She noted that he was rather nervous * Note my words!

2 **note** He spoke without notes ALSO: take notes (Notizen machen) * bank-note *(Banknote)*

3 **once** She goes to see her aunt once a week *(einmal in der Woche)* ALSO: He once lived in Paris *(früher einmal)* * Once you know him better you'11 understand him *(sobald / wenn du ihn besser kennst)* * I stopped smoking once and for all *(ein für allemal)*

4 **once in a while** They go to the movies once in a while

5 **at once** Come here at once * He reacted at once SYN: immediately

6 **major** a major problem, operation, road etc. * of major importance *(von großer Bedeutung)* ALSO: C major *(C-Dur)* NOUN: major *(der Major)* BUT: mayor *(der Bürgermeister)*

7 **original** an original plan, reason, inhabitant etc. ALSO: an original idea *(originelle Idee)* NOUN: This painting is an original

8 **staff** staff officer (Stabsoffizier) * staff costs (Personalkosten) VERB: The office was understaffed *(unterbesetzt)*

9 **compel** They compelled him to confess *(zwangen ihn zu gestehen)* SYN: force

10 **bore** He bored me with his endless talks * They were bored by his silly jokes * That bores me to death NOUN: He's a real bore *(Langweiler)*

11 **safe** a safe place, speed, dog etc.; In the house they were safe from the rain *(sicher vor)*

12 **intention** They have no intention of moving house *(nicht die Absicht umzuziehen)* * His intentions are good but he should also carry them out *(seine Vorsätze)*

13 **healthy** a healthy person, climate, appetite etc.

14 **prediction** SYN: forecast VERB: The meteorologists predict an unpleasant summer

15 **offence** an offence against good manners, God, regulations, the law etc. ALSO: Offence is the best defence *(Angriff ist die beste Verteidigung)* ADJ: offensive *(offensiv, anstößig)*

16 **neck** He could save bis neck *(seinen Hals retten)* * Don't break your neck!

17 **tie** family ties, business ties, ties of friendship * tie up a parcel *(Packet verschnüren)* * tie someone's hands together *(fesseln)* ALSO: I can't come, I am too tied up with my examination *(zu sehr in Anspruch genommen)* * He usually wears a tie *(trägt eine Krawatte)*

18 **wrap** Please wrap it up in paper ALSO: I wrapped myself up before going out into the cold *(zog mich warm an)*

19 **succeed** He succeeded in crossing the river * She succeeded in life OPP: to fail

20 **issue** They argued political issues * issues of coins, stamps, magazines etc.

21 **appreciate** I don't appreciate foreign food * I appreciate that this will cause problems for you * His help wasn't appreciated

honest ['ɒnɪst]	*ehrlich, aufrichtig*	[1]
to acquire	*erwerben, erlangen*	[2]
payment	*Bezahlung; Vergütung*	
inferior [ɪn'fɪərɪə]	*untergeordnet; minderwertig*	[3]
taste	*schmecken (nach); Geschmack*	[4]
however	*jedoch, aber; wie auch immer*	[5]
low [ləʊ]	*niedrig; tief; leise (Stimme)*	
to take into account	*berücksichtigen*	
outline	*Umriss; Skizze*	[6]
noble	*adlig; großzügig; edel*	
to drop	*tropfen; fallen (lassen);*	[7]
to confirm	*bestätigen; bekräftigen*	[8]
lazy	*faul; träge*	[9]
to raise [reɪz]	*(hoch-/ auf-) heben*	[10]
rise [raɪz]	*(Gehalts-) Erhöhung*	
to sail (for)	*segeln; abfahren (nach)*	[11]
to preserve	*erhalten; bewahren*	[12]
earnings	*Einkommen; Arbeitslohn*	
to rush	*drängen; rasen*	[13]
to state	*darlegen; festsetzen*	
minor	*kleiner; unbedeutend*	[14]
tool	*Werkzeug; Gerät*	[15]
in the long run	*auf die Dauer*	[16]
to run for	*kandidieren für*	[17]
to run out	*zu Ende gehen*	[18]
to run	*laufen; führen, leiten*	[19]
for the sake of	*um ... willen*	[20]
vital ['vaɪtl]	*(lebens)wichtig; wesentlich*	
reputation [ˌrepjʊ'teɪʃn]	*Ruf; Ansehen*	[21]

1 **honest** Please give me your honest opinion. NOUN: honesty *(Ehrlichkeit, Aufrichtigkeit)*

2 **acquire** to acquire knowledge, to acquire a reputation

3 **inferior** She had to work in an inferior position * The food was of inferior quality superior

4 **taste** She tasted the soup; it tasted of salt NOUN: Sugar has a sweet taste * By buying that green hat she showed her bad taste

5 **however** Afterwards, however, he was quite exhausted *(Danach war er jedoch ganz erschöpft)* * They couldn't persuade her, however hard they tried *(so sehr sie sich auch bemühten)*

6 **outline** He gave an outline of the story *(gab die Geschichte in groben Zügen wieder)* * Before he began with the painting, he drew up an outline *(fertigte eine Skizze an)*. VERB: to outline *(skizzieren, umreißen)*

7 **drop** He dropped the cup *(ließ die Tasse fallen)* * She dropped to the ground *(fiel zu Boden)* ALSO: to drop a subject, a habit, an idea etc. * They dropped in for a cup of tea *(schauten herein, kamen vorbei)*

8 **confirm** They only believed the news when it was confirmed by a Government spokesman * His behaviour confirmed me in my opinion of him

9 **lazy** NOUN: laziness *(Faulheit)* NOTE: lazy-bones *(Faulpelz)*

10 **raise** raise a glass, prices etc. BUT: the prices rise *(steigen)* ALSO: raise a problem *(aufwerfen)*; raise children *(aufziehen)*

11 **sail** They sailed their own boat * He has sailed for France *(ist nach Frankreich abgefahren)*

12 **preserve** preserve food *(einmachen)*, preserve the natural environment *(bewahren)*, animals *(präparieren)*; preserve children from brutal films

13 **rush** The police rushed to the scene of the crime * Don't rush me, I need more time!

14 **minor** minor repairs, problems, injuries etc. * of minor importance *(von geringer Bedeutung)* ALSO: C minor *(c-moll)* NOUN: At 17 she is still a minor *(ist sie noch nicht volljährig)*

15 **tool** e.g. spanner *(Schraubenschlüssel)*, screwdriver *(Schraubenzieher)*, pincers *(Zange)*, drill *(Bohrer)*, scissors *(Schere)* etc. ALSO: computer tools *(Hilfsprogramme)*

16 **in the long run** Being kind towards others pays in the long run *(zahlt sich auf Dauer aus)*

17 **run for** He was running for president/for mayor *(kandidierte für das Präsidenten-/Bürgermeisteramt)*

18 **run out** North Sea oil will run out in a few decades * We had run out of petrol *(war uns ausgegangen)*

19 **run** He ran a good race *(lief)* * She ran the shop quite successfully *(führte)* ALSO: He ran the risk/danger of being shot *(ging das Risiko ein / lief Gefahr)*

20 **for the sake of** They did it for the sake of peace *(um des Friedens willen)*

21 **reputation** She has a good reputation * a man of high reputation

honour	['ɒnə]	*Ehre*	[1]
human	['hjuːmən]	*menschlich*	[2]
human being		*Mensch*	
humane	[hjuː'meɪn]	*human; menschenfreundlich*	[3]
to intervene	[ˌɪntə'viːn]	*einschreiten*	[4]
to operate		*bedienen; operieren*	[5]
statement		*Darstellung; Behauptung*	[6]
manpower		*Arbeitskräfte*	
altogether		*vollkommen; insgesamt*	[7]
to seem		*scheinen*	[8]
thus	[ðʌs]	*so; auf diese Weise*	[9]
to search		*suchen; durchsuchen*	[10]
coarse	[kɔːs]	*grob; rauh*	[11]
to exaggerate		*übertreiben*	
vivid		*lebhaft; lebendig*	[12]
to ease		*lindern; erleichtern*	[13]
racial	['reɪʃəl]	*rassisch; Rassen -*	
employment		*Beschäftigung; Arbeit; Beruf*	
salary		*Gehalt*	[14]
to do without		*entbehren (können)*	[15]
pure	['pjʊə]	*echt; rein*	[16]
misery		*Elend; Not*	[17]
suspicion	[sə'spiʃn]	*Verdacht; Argwohn*	[18]
pollutant		*Schadstoff*	[19]
agriculture		*Landwirtschaft*	
host		*Gastgeber*	[20]
to seize	[sɪːz]	*packen, ergreifen; beschlagnahmen*	[21]
reluctance	[rɪ'lʌktəns]	*Abneigung; Widerwillen*	[22]

1 **honour** It is a question of honour * She had the honour of opening the exhibition * They celebrated in his honour *(ihm zu Ehren)* VERB: to honour *(ehren)*

2 **human** the human brain, the human nature * She tried all that is humanly possible

3 **humane** a humane character, employer, treatment etc.

4 **intervene** At last he intervened in their dispute. ALSO: I will arrive by midday if nothing intervenes *(wenn nichts dazwischen kommt)*

5 **operate** She is the only one who can operate the machine * They had to operate the patient ALSO: The machine wasn't operating properly *(arbeitete nicht richtig)* * This train is operated by electricity *(ist elektrizitätsbetrieben)*

6 **statement** NOTE: bank statement *(Kontoauszug)* * to make a statement *(eine Aussage machen)*

7 **altogether** They had altogether failed SYN: completely * We paid £ 20 altogether *(insgesamt)* BUT: We sang this song all together *(alle zusammen)*

8 **seem** He seems to be interested * It seems easy to her, but difficult to me

9 **thus** He managed to get into the lifeboat and thus he saved his life SYN: in this way

10 **search** I searched through all my books * The police searched for the thief *(suchten ihn)* * Having been found he was searched *(durchsucht)*

11 **coarse** coarse sand, cloth, jokes, manners etc.

12 **vivid** a vivid colour * He gave a vivid description of his adventures

13 **ease** The doctor eased him of his pain *(befreite ihn von)* ALSO: to ease up *(nachlassen)* His pain eased up slowly * The wind eased up

14 **salary** a monthly, quarterly salary; a salary per annum BUT: a weekly wage *(Wochenlohn)*

15 **do without** Yesterday we had to do without his help *(mussten ohne seine Hilfe auskommen)*

16 **pure** pure gold, air, thoughts etc. * a pure waste of time *(reine Zeitverschwendung)*

17 **misery** ADJ: miserable lives of poor people, miserable slums, a miserable meal, weather etc.

18 **suspicion** VERB: to suspect *(verdächtigen; vermuten)* * He was suspected of murder *(Er wurde des Mordes verdächtigt)* * We had always suspected that she would lose her money one day *(vermutet / erwartet)*

19 **pollutant** NOUN: pollution *(Verschmutzung)* VERB: Many factories pollute the environment *(verschmutzen die Umwelt)*

20 **host** He has always been a good host NOTE: host *(Quizmaster, Talkmaster)* He is the successful host of a game show NOTE: hostess *(Gastgeberin etc.)*

21 **seize** to seize a thief, an opportunity * He was seized by fear BUT: to cease (aufhören)

22 **reluctance** His reluctance to help us was quite obvious ADJ: She seemed reluctant to seize her chance

root	[ruːt]	*Wurzel* [1]	
pleasant	[ˈpleznt]	*angenehm* [2]	pleasure
to supply (with)		*versorgen (mit); liefern* [3]	
communications		*Nachrichtenwesen*	
to mourn (for)	[mɔːn]	*trauern (um)*	
glance	[glɑːns]	*flüchtiger Blick* [4]	
at a glance		*auf den ersten Blick*	at first sight
to stretch		*dehnen, strecken; sich erstrecken*	
to rely on		*sich verlassen auf*	to depend on
witness		*Zeuge* [5]	
training		*Ausbildung; Training* [6]	physical exercise
vocation		*Beruf* [7]	
to apply (to)		*anwenden (auf)* [8]	
origin	[ˈɒridʒɪn]	*Ursprung; Herkunft* [9]	
strength		*Stärke; Kraft*	to strengthen
to intend		*beabsichtigen* [10]	intention
to be intended for		*bestimmt sein für* [11]	
peril		*Gefahr*	perilous
to strip		*abstreifen; ausziehen* [12]	
to offend		*beleidigen* [13]	to insult
health		*Gesundheit* [14]	
alien	[ˈeɪlɪən]	*fremd; ausländisch; Ausländer* [15]	
to obey (s.o.)	[əˈbeɪ]	*(jemd.) gehorchen; befolgen* [16]	
alive	[əˈlaɪv]	*lebendig; lebend* [17]	
to excite	[ɪkˈsaɪt]	*erregen; aufregen; hervorrufen* [18]	
belt		*Gürtel; Treibriemen* [19]	
to deteriorate	[dɪˈtɪərɪəreɪt]	*schlechter werden; sich verschlechtern* [20]	
to commit		*begehen* [21]	
domestic		*häuslich; Inlands-* [22]	home

to tease

1 **root** the root of a plant, a hair, a problem NOTE: square root *(Quadratwurzel)*

2 **pleasant** a pleasant visitor, evening, meal, journey etc.

3 **supply** The hungry men were supplied with food * She couldn't supply the information that was needed NOUN: He usually has a good supply of cigarettes in his car *(Vorrat)*

4 **glance** VERB: He glanced round the room *(Er blickte sich kurz im Zimmer um)*

5 **witness** NOTE: eye-witness, ear-witness; to give witness *(Zeugnis ablegen)* VERB: They witnessed a terrible car crash *(wurden Zeuge)*

6 **training** VERB: to train a child (to be a good citizen), a person (for a job), an animal (for the circus or a race)

7 **vocation** ALSO: He has no vocation for his profession *(ist für seinen Beruf nicht geeignet)* ADJ: vocational training *(Berufsausbildung);* vocational adviser *(Berufsberater)*

8 **apply** We could apply her findings in our work * The rule was applied ALSO: That doesn't apply to you *(trifft nicht auf dich zu)* * He applied the brakes of his car *(zog die Bremse an)*

9 **origin** the origin of civilization, a quarrel, people, goods etc.

10 **intend** ALSO: Is this picture intended to be Tom? *(soll das Tom sein?)* * This is my intended *(meine Zukünftige/mein Zukünftiger)*

11 **be intended** This remark was not intended for you * This park is intended for everybody

12 **strip** NOUN: strip *(Streifen; schmales Stück)* NOTE: strip cartoon *(Comic)*

13 **offend** to offend a person, the ear, the eye ALSO: That offends against the law *(verstößt gegen das Gesetz)*

14 **health** He is in good / poor health *(bei guter /schlechter Gesundheit)*

15 **alien** Dishonesty was completely alien to his nature VERB: to alienate *(entfremden)*

16 **obey** soldiers must obey orders NOUN: obedience [ə'bɪːdɪəns] *(Gehorsam)*

17 **alive** to stay alive *(am Leben bleiben)* * Wanted, dead or alive! * He is the greatest poet alive *(der größte lebende Dichter)*

18 **excite** Don't excite yourself * He said nothing to get excited about *(nichts, worüber man sich aufregen müsste)* * They excited a rebellion *(verursachten einen Aufstand)*

19 **belt** the belt of trousers, a green belt round a town, a safety belt *(Sicherheitsgurt)*, a conveyor belt *(Förderband)*

20 **deteriorate** The economy / the house / the road / deteriorated rapidly

21 **commit** to commit a crime, a murder, suicide *(Selbstmord)* etc. NOTE: a committed teacher *(ein engagierter Lehrer)*

22 **domestic** He is a very domestic person ALSO: domestic servant *(Hausangestellter)*, domestic animal *(Haustier)*, domestic flights *(Inlandsflüge)*, domestic policy *(Innenpolitik)*

to issue		*herausgeben; austeilen*	[1]
success		*Erfolg*	
bill		*Rechnung;(Geld)Schein;Gesetzentwurf*	
pale (with)		*blass (vor)*	[2]
to encounter		*treffen, stoßen auf*	[3]
to melt		*schmelzen; schwinden*	[4]
liquid		*flüssig; Flüssigkeit*	
to greet		*(be)grüßen*	[5]
actual		*wirklich, tatsächlich*	[6]
to pour	[pɔː]	*(er)gießen; einschenken*	[7]
temper		*Temperament; Stimmung*	[8]
object	['ɒbdʒɪkt]	*Gegenstand; Ziel*	[9]
to wipe		*(ab)wischen; abtrocknen*	[10]
true		*wahr; echt*	
to come true		*sich bewahrheiten*	[11]
ugly	['ʌglɪ]	*häßlich*	[12]
hazard	['hæzəd]	*Gefahr; Wagnis*	[13]
striking		*auffallend; eindrucksvoll*	[14]
pool		*Teich, Tümpel; (Spiel-)Einsatz*	[15]
inferiority	[ɪnˌfɪərɪ'ɒrɪtɪ]	*Minderwertigkeit; Unterlegenheit*	[16]
comprehensive		*umfassend*	[17]
efficiency	[ɪ'fɪʃənsɪ]	*Tüchtigkeit; Leistungsfähigkeit*	
to retaliate	[rɪ'tælɪeɪt]	*vergelten; sich rächen*	[18]
tax		*Steuer; besteuern*	
majority / minority		*Mehrheit / Minderheit*	
rough	[rʌf]	*rauh; grob; stürmisch*	[19]
roughly		*ungefähr; annähernd*	[20]
council		*Rat(sversammlung); Beratung*	[21]
secret	['sɪːkrɪt]	*geheim; versteckt; Geheimnis*	

1 **issue** to issue a magazine, a newspaper etc. * Warm clothes were issued to the victims of the catastrophe *(wurden an die Opfer der Katastrophe ausgegeben)*

2 **pale** He turned pale at the news *(wurde blass angesichts der Nachricht)*

3 **encounter** to encounter problems, difficulties, an obstacle *(Hindernis)* * The other day I encountered an old friend of mine *(traf ihn zufällig)*

4 **melt** the melting of snow, money, resources * a crowd melts away *(löst sich auf)* ALSO: My heart melted with pity when I saw her cry

5 **greet** They don't greet each other * The news was greeted with great joy NOUN: greeting *(Gruß, Begrüßung)*

6 **actual** Quarrelling about unimportant details they forgot about the actual problem BUT: a topical problem *(aktuelles Problem)* * That's no longer relevant *(nicht mehr aktuell)* * a current affairs programme *(aktuelle Sendung)*

7 **pour** The fans poured out of the stadium * He poured himself a cup of tea * pouring rain *(strömender Regen)*

8 **temper** NOTE: He kept/lost his temper *(beherrschte sich / verlor die Beherrschung)* * She was out of temper with him *(war ihm böse)*

9 **object** Various objects were lying on the table * She has always been an object of admiration * His only object was to become president

10 **wipe** to wipe the floor, one's nose, something dry etc. ALSO: to wipe out *(auslöschen)* * In the course of Napoleon's Russian campaign almost his entire army was wiped out

11 **come true** In the end all their dreams came true *(wurden wahr)*

12 **ugly** an ugly person, scene, wound, foul etc.

13 **hazard** health hazard *(Gesundheitsrisiko)* * VERB: Racing drivers often hazard their lives *(riskieren ihr Leben/ setzen ihr Leben aufs Spiel)*

14 **striking** a striking performance, record, beauty etc. BUT: striking workers = workers who are on strike

15 **pool** NOTE: She won on the pools *(im Toto)* * car-pool *(Fahrgemeinschaft)* * pool-room *(Billardzimmer)*

16 **inferiority** inferiority complex *(Minderwertigkeitskomplex)*

17 **comprehensive** She made a comprehensive report of what had happened NOTE: comprehensive school *(Gesamtschule)*

18 **retaliate** They retaliated upon their enemies *(rächten sich an)* NOUN: an act of retaliation *(Vergeltungsmaßnahme)*

19 **rough** a rough cloth, child, behaviour,sea etc.

20 **roughly** The pool was roughly 50 yards away SYN: approximately BUT: He was treated roughly *(wurde grob behandelt)*

21 **council** ALSO: councillor *(Ratsmitglied)* * to be in council *(beraten)*

odd		*seltsam; einzeln; ungerade* [1]
to retire		*sich zurückziehen; zurücktreten; in den Ruhestand treten* [2]
eager	[ˈiːgə]	*begierig; eifrig* [3]
to force		*zwingen* [4]
force		*Gewalt; Stärke; Macht*
indispensable		*unentbehrlich* [5]
to tackle		*anpacken, in Angriff nehmen* [6]
heel	[ˈhiːl]	*Ferse; Absatz* [7]
to prohibit	[prəˈhɪbɪt]	*verbieten* [8]
voyage	[ˈvɔɪɪdʒ]	*Seereise; Fahrt im Weltraum* [9]
due	[djuː]	*fällig* [10]
due to		*infolge*
care		*Sorgfalt* [11]
to take care		*sich Mühe geben; sich hüten* [12]
to take care of		*sorgen für; erledigen* [13]
economical		*sparsam; wirtschaftlich* [14]
economic		*(volks)wirtschaftlich; Wirtschafts-*
economy	[ɪˈkɒnəmɪ]	*Wirtschaft(ssystem); Sparsamkeit*
economics	[ɪkəˈnɒmɪks]	*Wirtschaftswissenschaften; Volkswirtschaft* [15]
detrimental		*schädlich* [16]
failure	[ˈfeɪljə]	*Misserfolg; Versagen; Versager* [17]
main		*hauptsächlich* [18]
in the main		*im Großen und Ganzen*
incentive		*Anreiz, Ansporn; Antrieb* [19]
to wave		*wehen, flattern; winken* [20]
goal	[gəʊl]	*Ziel; Tor* [21]
to assume	[əˈsjuːm]	*annehmen; voraussetzen* [22]

1 **odd** an odd person, appearance, event SYN: strange * What's the use of an odd shoe? *(einzeln)* * An odd number cannot exactly be divided by two NOTE: She hadn't seen them for twenty-odd years *(seit über zwanzig Jahren)*

2 **retire** They retired early *(zogen sich früh zum Schlafen zurück)* * The enemy retired *(zog sich zurück)* * Under the pressure of the public the minister retired *(trat zurück)* * He retired on a pension *(trat in den Ruhestand)*

3 **eager** She is eager for admiration *(begierig nach Bewunderung)* * an eager learner * an eager beaver *(Streber;* beaver = *Biber)*

4 **force** They opened the door by force * They forced the door open * the police force, the forces of nature * gale force 10 *(Windstärke 10)*

5 **indispensable** food is indispensable to life *(lebensnotwendig)*

6 **tackle** to tackle a piece of work, a problem, a meal

7 **heel** They were on my heels *(Sie waren mir auf den Fersen)* BUT: to heal *(heilen)*

8 **prohibit** The spitting on the floor is prohibited SYN: forbid NOUN: prohibition *(gesetzliches Verbot, insbesondere von Alkohol)*

9 **voyage** They were on the voyage out / home *(auf der Hin- / Rückreise)*

10 **due** The train is due to arrive at 6 p.m. * When is the baby due? ALSO: He came in due course *(im rechten Augenblick)*

11 **care** Please do it with more care * Handle the toy with care

12 **take care** Take care not to drop that plate *(Pass auf, dass du den Teller nicht fallen lässt)*

13 **take care of** At the weekend his wife takes care of the kids * She always takes care of the details

14 **economical** This car is economical of energy *(geht sparsam mit Energie um)* VERB: to economize *(sparsam sein)*

15 **economics** NOTE: economist *(Wirtschaftswissenschaftler)*

16 **detrimental** This statement is detrimental to my interests * The detrimental effects of pollution

17 **failure** Our weekend trip was a complete failure * Due to the failure of the brakes he lost control of the car * He proved to be a failure *(erwies sich als Versager)*

18 **main** SYN: chief NOTE: the mains *(Stromnetz)* * This recorder is mains operated *(für Netzbetrieb bestimmt)*

19 **incentive** The good mark was an incentive to work even harder * He hasn't much incentive

20 **wave** The flag waved in the wind * She waved to me as she passed *(winkte mir zu, während sie vorbeiging)*

21 **goal** She has achieved all her goals * He scored a goal *(schoss ein Tor)*

22 **assume** Let's assume you know the answer * As he isn't here yet, I assume he isn't coming ALSO: assuming that *(angenommen, dass)*

objection	[əb'dʒekʃn]	*Einwand; Einspruch*	[1]
thirst	[θɜːst]	*Durst*	
several		*mehrere; verschiedene*	
respect		*Achtung; Hinsicht*	[2]
to apply for		*sich bewerben um*	[3]
purpose	['pɜːpəs]	*Zweck; Absicht*	[4]
on purpose		*absichtlich*	
feature	['fiːtʃə]	*Kennzeichen; (Gesichts-/Charakter)zug*	[5]
to guide	[gaɪd]	*führen, lenken*	[6]
shame		*Schande*	[7]
term		*Zeitraum; Semester; Fachausdruck*	[8]
terms		*Bedingungen*	[9]
to enlarge		*vergrößern*	[10]
desire		*Wunsch, Sehnsucht*	[11]
usual	[juːʒl]	*gewöhnlich*	[12]
to advocate		*befürworten*	[13]
to cope (with)		*gewachsen sein, fertig werden mit*	[14]
to rule		*(be)herrschen*	[15]
store		*Lager, Vorrat*	[16]
event	[ɪ'vent]	*Ereignis; Veranstaltung*	[17]
conscious	['kɒnʃəs]	*bewusst*	[18]
knowledge	['nɒlɪdʒ]	*Wissen; Kenntnis*	[19]
equal	['iːkwəl]	*gleich; gleichkommen*	[20]
strange		*fremd; sonderbar, merkwürdig*	[21]
disaster		*Unheil; Katastrophe*	
to wonder (at)	['wʌndə]	*sich wundern (über); sich fragen*	[22]
giant	[dʒaɪənt]	*Riese; riesig*	
link		*Verbindung*	[23]
to restrict		*einschränken, beschränken*	

1 **objection** I have no objection to it ALSO: She had a strong objection to cheap restaurants *(Abneigung)*

2 **respect** They showed great respect for her work * He is a true friend in all respects *(in jeder Hinsicht)* ALSO: We must make our plans with respect to future needs *(im Hinblick auf)*

3 **apply** I applied for the position NOUN: application *(Bewerbung)*

4 **purpose** What is the purpose of this tool? * It was not my purpose to offend you ALSO: He worked hard but to no purpose *(ohne Ergebnis/Erfolg)*

5 **feature** features of a district, project etc. * She has coarse features *(grobe Gesichtszüge)*

6 **guide** NOUN: a guide *(Führer, als Person oder in Buchform)* * We were shown round the cathedral by a guide

7 **shame** He brought shame on his parents * He felt shame at having told her a lie NOTE: to be ashamed of *(sich einer Sache schämen)*

8 **term** a term of seven years * term of notice *(Kündigungsfrist)*

9 **terms** terms of payment /surrender *(Zahlungs-/Kapitulations-bedingungen)* NOTE; to be on good terms *(auf gutem Fuß stehen)* * to come to terms with *(sich einigen mit)*

10 **enlarge** to enlarge a photograph, a building, a garden etc.

11 **desire** a desire for peace * I have no desire to see them VERB: to desire *(wünschen, begehren)*

12 **usual** The train was late as usual * She usually gets up early

13 **advocate** She advocates a radical reform * Do you advocate a ban on smoking?

14 **cope** to cope with a person, difficulties, a problem SYN: to manage * Can you manage? *(Kommst du zurecht?)*

15 **rule** to rule over an empire; to rule a partner ALSO: She was ruled by jealousy *(von Eifersucht besessen)*

16 **store** We have a large number of hats in store *(auf Lager)* * Nobody knows what the future has in store *(was die Zukunft bringt)*

17 **event** NOTE: at all events *(auf alle Fälle)*

18 **conscious** He wasn't conscious of her being absent * He was knocked out but he's now conscious again *(wieder bei Bewusstsein)* NOUN: consciousness

19 **knowledge** NOTE: to the best of my knowledge she is still on holiday *(soweit ich weiß)*

20 **equal** The cake was divided into 12 equal parts * There is no-one to equal her in intelligence ALSO: He didn't feel equal to the problem *(war dem Problem nicht* gewachsen)

21 **strange** ALSO: He was strange to hard work *(nicht gewohnt)*

22 **wonder** I don't wonder at this accident * I was wondering what to say NOUN: Small wonder he was embarrassed *(kein Wunder, dass er verlegen war)* BUT: It was a miracle that he wasn't killed in the accident

23 **link** a rail link, the link of a chain *(Kettenglied)*, a link between smoking and cancer VERB: to link *(verbinden, in Verbindung bringen)*

surface	['sɜːfɪs]	*Oberfläche*
responsible (for)		*verantwortlich (für)* [1]
to account for		*erklären* [2]
to keep up with		*Schritt halten mit* [3]
to keep in mind		*sich merken; denken an*
late		*spät; verspätet; verstorben* [4]
latest		*neuest, jüngst* [5]
to check		*überprüfen, kontrollieren* [6]
elaborate	[ɪ'læbərət]	*sorgfältig ausgearbeitet* [7] sophisticate
crucial	['kruːʃl]	*kritisch, ernst; entscheidend* [8] critical, decisive
poison		*Gift; vergiften*
sincere	[sɪn'sɪə]	*aufrichtig* Yours sincerely
to owe	[əʊ]	*schulden; verdanken* [9]
pain		*Schmerz* [10]
to surround		*umgeben* [11]
efficient	[ɪ'fɪʃənt]	*wirkungsvoll; tüchtig* [12]
to comprehend		*verstehen, begreifen; einschließen* [13]
to postpone	[pə'spəʊn]	*verschieben, aufschieben* [14]
evil	['iːvl] bad, nasty	*schlimm; böse; Übel* [15]
advantage , benefit		*Vorteil, Nutzen*
to take advantage of		*ausnutzen, Vorteil ziehen aus*
disadvantage		*Nachteil; Schaden*
suitable	['suːtəbl]	*passend, geeignet* [16]
to object (to)	[əb'dʒekt]	*Einspruch erheben (gegen)* [17]
wave		*Welle, Woge* [18]
to store		*aufbewahren; speichern* [19]
rule		*Regel; Herrschaft* [20]
as a rule		*in der Regel*
to affect	/effect	*beeinflussen; in Mitleidenschaft ziehen* [21]

1 **responsible** He was responsible for the organization of the festival ALSO: a responsible job *(verantwortungsvoll)* NOUN: You do it on your own responsibility *(auf eigene Verantwortung)*

2 **account for** That accounts for it *(das ist die Erklärung dafür)* ALSO: There is no accounting for tastes *(über Geschmack läßt sich nicht streiten)*

3 **keep up with** She can't keep up with him *(kann nicht mit ihm mithalten)* BUT: Don't keep me up *(Halte mich nicht auf!)*

4 **late** She arrived late *(verspätete sich)* * The late mayor *(der verstorbene Bürgermeister)* NOTE: He has been rather absent-minded of late *(in letzter Zeit)*

5 **latest** the latest hits *(die neuesten / letzten Hits)* BUT: 'let it be' was the Beatles' last record *(die letzte ihrer Platten)*

6 **check** At the border they checked our passports * Please check the oil and the tyres! BUT: to control *(Kontrolle haben über, Kontrolle ausüben)* She couldn't control herself *(verlor die Selbstbeherrschung)* * He lost control over the car

7 **elaborate** an elaborate technique, machine, system etc.

8 **crucial** at the crucial moment * the crucial question

9 **owe** He owes him ten pounds * He owed much to her *(verdankte ihr viel)*

10 **pain** to feel some/ cry with/ be in pain ADJ: painful *(schmerzhaft)*; painless *(schmerzlos)* NOTE: to take pains *(sich Mühe geben)*

11 **surround** They were surrounded by the enemy * Many trees surround the castle * She is surrounded by many sincere friends NOUN: surroundings *(die Umgebung)*

12 **efficient** an efficient method; an efficient manager * He worked rather efficiently

13 **comprehend** He heard the words but couldn't comprehend them * A good education comprehends love and patience

14 **postpone** to postpone a meeting, the writing of a letter etc.

15 **evil** NOTE: the lesser of two evils *(das kleinere Übel)* * an evil-doer *(Übeltäter)* * evil-minded *(boshaft, hämisch)*

16 **suitable** VERB: to suit *(passen; geeignet sein)* * Will Monday suit you? *(Passt es dir am Montag?)* * The shirt really suits him *(steht ihm gut)* BUT: The coat doesn't fit *(passt nicht)*

17 **object** Father always objects when I am late *(protestiert)* * I objected to being treated like a child * She objected that nobody would be able to pay for it *(sie wandte ein)*

18 **wave** the waves of the sea, radio waves, permanent waves *(Dauerwellen)*, a wave of sympathy *(eine Welle des Mitleids)*

19 **store** He stored his old rifle away * He stored up a good supply of coal for the winter

20 **rule** the rules of chess *(Schachregeln)* * The rule of Henry VIII * It's my rule to smoke a pipe after dinner *(Gewohnheit)*

21 **affect** This decision will affect your career * The area was affected by drought *(von Dürre befallen)* NOUN: affection *(Zuneigung, Liebe)*

to observe		*beobachten; bemerken*	[1]
to appear		*erscheinen; scheinen*	[2]
wage(s)		*Lohn*	[3]
violent	[ˈvaɪelənt]	*heftig; gewalttätig*	[4]
occasion		*Gelegenheit; Anlass*	[5]
worth	[wɜːθ]	*Wert*	[6]
to adopt		*annehmen; übernehmen*	[7]
offer		*anbieten; Angebot*	
to steer		*steuern*	[8]
calm		*ruhig; still*	[9]
to last		*dauern; (aus)reichen*	[10]
rural		*ländlich*	
currency		*Währung*	
to occupy	[ˈɒkjʊpaɪ]	*in Anspruch nehmen; besetzen*	[11]
to guess	[ges]	*(er)raten; vermuten*	[12]
pipe		*Pfeife; Leitung; Röhre*	[13]
acquaintance		*Bekanntschaft; Bekannter*	[14]
to rub (against)		*reiben (an)*	
support		*unterstützen; ernähren; Unterstützung; Hilfe*	[15]
to value	[ˈvæljuː]	*bewerten; schätzen*	[16]
sound		*klingen; Ton; Schall*	
track		*(Fuß)spur; Gleise*	[17]
to get rid of		*loswerden*	
to punish (for)		*bestrafen (für)*	
to examine		*prüfen; untersuchen; verhören*	[18]
beyond		*jenseits; über . . . hinaus*	[19]
beyond doubt		*zweifellos*	[20]
controversy	[ˈkɒntrəvɜːsi]	*Streit(frage)*	

1 **observe** to observe the stars, the enemy, a pretty girl in the crowd ALSO: He observed the doctor's instructions *(beachtete)*

2 **appear** The train appeared on the horizon * The peak appeared before us * The book will soon appear * It appears to me that he has forgotten it OPP: to disappear *(verschwinden)*

3 **wage** His wages are 120 pounds a week * wage claim *(Lohnforderung)*

4 **violent** a violent wind, toothache etc. * a violent attack, temper etc.

5 **occasion** I had few occasions to meet him * This is not an occasion for sadness ALSO: He had no occasion to regret what he had said *(keinen Grund)*

6 **worth** This watch is worth £ 500 * The book wasn't worth reading ALSO: the book wasn't worth while reading NOUN: an item of some, great, little worth

7 **adopt** to adopt a name, a method, an idea, a custom etc. ALSO: to adopt a child *(adoptieren)*

8 **steer** to steer a boat, ship, car NOTE: steering wheel *(Steuer-/Lenkrad)*

9 **calm** a calm lake, sea, passage, person; calm weather VERB: to calm down *(beruhigen, sich beruhigen)*

10 **last** the rain/ an illness/ my love may last long * The water lasted only for two days *(reichte aus)* * This coat will last several years *(halten)*

11 **occupy** to occupy a house, room, seat, position, etc. * Writing letters occupied his free time * They occupied the enemy's territory *(besetzten)* * She was occupied with her children *(beschäftigt)*

12 **guess** to guess a secret, to guess what a person is thinking * I guess her to be 35 *(schätze sie auf)* NOUN: Your guess is as good as mine *(Ich weiß ebenso wenig wie du)*

13 **pipe** pipe of peace *(Friedenspfeife)* * water-pipes *(Wasserleitung)* * pipeline

14 **acquaintance** I made her acquaintance yesterday * She is not a friend, only an acquaintance

15 **support** She supported him in his struggle * Can you support a family? * He was so weak that they had to support him NOUN: supporter *(Anhänger)*

16 **value** They valued the car at 900 pounds * Do you value him as an employee? NOUN: the value of a piece of information, a book, a currency

17 **track** tracks in the snow * The train went off the track *(entgleiste)* * He was off the track *(auf dem Holzweg)*

18 **examine** The doctor examined the patient thoroughly * The police examined the suspect for three hours * the students will be examined in maths tomorrow

19 **beyond** They live beyond the valley * That goes beyond a joke * We stayed beyond midnight

20 **beyond doubt** ALSO: beyond belief *(unglaublich)*, beyond control *(außer Kontrolle)* * This watch is beyond repair *(lässt sich nicht mehr reparieren)*

appearance	*Anschein; Äußeres; Erscheinung*	[1]
fancy	*sich einbilden; glauben; Einbildungskraft; Laune*	[2]
to challenge	*herausfordern; verlangen; anzweifeln*	[3]
favour	*bevorzugen; begünstigen; Gefallen*	[4]
in favour of	*zugunsten*	[5]
defence	*Verteidigung*	
impression	*Eindruck*	[6]
to delay [dɪˈleɪ]	*aufhalten; verzögern*	[7]
need	*Bedürfnis; Not*	[8]
to look after	*aufpassen; sorgen für*	[9]
to look for	*suchen*	
to look forward to	*sich freuen auf*	[10]
to generate	*erzeugen*	[11]
prospects	*(Zukunfts-)Aussichten*	[12]
straight [streɪt]	*gerade; unmittelbar*	[13]
within [wɪˈðɪn]	*innerhalb*	[14]
tides	*Gezeiten*	[15]
equality [ɪˈkwɒlətɪ]	*Gleichheit*	
to overcome	*überwinden; überwältigen*	[16]
mystery [ˈmɪsterɪ]	*Geheimnis; Rätsel; Krimi*	[17]
to neglect	*vernachlässigen; versäumen*	[18]
sale	*Verkauf*	
dwelling	*Wohnung; Behausung*	
lock	*zuschließen, verschließen; Schloss*	[19]
branch	*Ast, Zweig*	[20]
gradually [ˈgrædjʊəlɪ]	*allmählich*	
to reply	*antworten*	[21]
licence [ˈlaɪsəns]	*Erlaubnis; Genehmigung*	

1 **appearance** to make an appearance *(sich zeigen)* * to judge by appearances *(nach dem Äußeren urteilen)* * She had a foreign appearance *(fremdländisches Äußeres)*

2 **fancy** Don't fancy you can fool me *(glaube ja nicht)* * the fancies of an artist *(Launen)*

3 **challenge** to challenge some-one to fight * They challenged the truth of my statement *(zweifelten an)*

4 **favour** The teacher favoured the pupil * Can you do me a favour? ALSO: I don't favour the idea *(halte nichts davon)*

5 **in favour of** He spoke in favour of me

6 **impression** I got an un-favourable impression of them

7 **delay** I was delayed by him * The train was delayed NOUN: the delay *(Aufschub; Verzögerung)* * There was a delay of five minutes

8 **need** His income could hardly satisfy his needs * It's good to have a friend in times of need

9 **look after** She is old enough to look after herself ALSO: They looked after the car *(schauten dem Auto nach)*

10 **look forward to** I was looking forward to the warm summer days * He was looking forward to seeing her again

11 **generate** to generate electricity, heat, power etc. * Loneliness sometimes generates despair NOUN: generation *(Erzeugung; Generation)*

12 **prospects** My prospects in my new job are excellent ALSO: From their new house they had a splendid prospect over the valley

13 **straight** a straight road * The drunken man wasn't able to walk straight * We had to go straight home because our father was waiting NOTE: I went straight ahead *(geradeaus)* * Please tell me straight away *(ohne Umschweife)*

14 **within** There was no tree within five miles * He returned within a minute * We heard a deep voice from within the house

15 **tides** The tide is in/out *(es ist Flut/Ebbe)* NOTE: low tide/ebb *(Ebbe)* * high tide/flood *(Flut)*

16 **overcome** to overcome a bad habit, the enemy, fear, etc. * I was overcome with loneliness *(von Einsamkeit überwältigt)*

17 **mystery** He made no mystery of his opinion ADJ: mysterious [mɪsˈtɪːəriəs] *(geheimnisvoll)*

18 **neglect** to neglect one's family, health, studies etc. * He neglected to tell us that the train would be delayed

19 **lock** NOTE: Don't forget your key, otherwise you'll be locked out *(ausgesperrt)* * She locked up her money in the safe *(sperrte es ein)*

20 **branch** ALSO: the branch of a river, railway line, road etc. * This bank has branches all over the town *(Zweigstellen)* * a branch of industry *(Industriezweig)* VERB: to branch off *(abzweigen)*

21 **reply** SYN: answer NOUN: in reply to your letter *(in Beantwor-tung Ihres Briefes)*

science		*(Natur-)Wissenschaft*
theatre		*Theater; Schauplatz; Operationssaal* [1]
wealth	[welθ]	*Reichtum; Wohlstand*
scarcely		*kaum* [2]
then		*dann (adv); folglich (conj); damals* [3]
by then		*bis dahin* [4]
ability		*Fähigkeit; Begabung* [5]
spacious	['speɪʃəs]	*geräumig*
occupation	[ˌɒkjʊ'peɪʃn]	*Beschäftigung; Beruf; Besetzung* [6]
to connect		*verbinden* [7]
to shape		*formen; gestalten* [8]
to be about to		*im Begriff sein zu* [9]
to select		*auswählen*
living		*Lebensunterhalt* [10]
probable		*wahrscheinlich*
to execute		*ausführen, durchführen; hinrichten* 11]
neither		*keine(r,s) von beiden* [12]
neither . . . nor		*weder . . . noch* [13]
load		*(be)laden; belasten; Ladung* [14]
to surprise		*überraschen; Überraschung* [15]
liberty		*Freiheit* [16]
to roar		*brüllen; tosen* [17]
art		*Kunst* [18]
volume	['vɒljuːm]	*der Band; Umfang; Volumen* [19]
to suppose		*vermuten; voraussetzen* [20]
thought	[θɔːt]	*Gedanke* [21]
envy	['envɪ]	*Neid; beneiden* [22]
disabled		*behindert; die Behinderten*
torture	['tɔːtʃə]	*Folter; foltern* [23]

1 **theatre** All Europe was a theatre of war *(Kriegsschauplatz)*

2 **scarcely** I scarcely know him * I had scarcely entered his room when he shouted at me

3 **then** We saw a film and then went to a restaurant * This isn't your glass? What is yours then? * Life was much easier then (in those days) * Mr. Ford, the then President ... *(der damalige Präsident)*

4 **by then** NOTE: now and then/again *(ab und zu)* SYN: occasionally

5 **ability** He is a man of great ability/abilities *(Fähigkeit, Begabung)* NOTE: I helped him to the best of my ability *(so gut ich konnte)*

6 **occupation** Stamp-collecting is a leisurely occupation * He has a profitable occupation * the occupation of enemy territory

7 **connect** towns are connected by roads, people are connected with a firm, by marriage, etc.

8 **shape** to shape pots of clay, one's future, a thought etc. NOUN: shape *(Form, Gestalt)*

9 **be about to** They were about to leave *(wollten gerade gehen)*

10 **living** He makes a living as a waiter *(verdient sich seinen Lebens-unterhalt)*

11 **execute** It will be difficult to execute their plan SYN: carry out * Prisoners used to be executed in public

12 **neither** She knew neither of them * Neither plan is reasonable

13 **neither ... nor** Neither she nor I could kill the animal

14 **load** to load parcels on a lorry, a lot of work onto one's employees NOUN: a lorry-load of sand * a heavy load on my shoulders *(schwere Verantwortung)*

15 **surprise** What a surprise! * He looked at me in surprise * The police surprised the burglar as he was about to leave the house

16 **liberty** the liberty of speech, of the press * He took the liberty of leaving *(nahm sich die Freiheit heraus zu gehen)* * They defended their liberty

17 **roar** a lion, the sea, traffic roars NOUN: a roar of laughter/ of rage

18 **art** NOTE: the fine arts *(die schönen Künste)* * a work of art *(Kunstwerk)* * artist *(Künstler)* BUT: It's a piece of cake! / That's easy! *(Das ist keine Kunst!)*

19 **volume** The dictionary consists of two volumes * the volume of a business * His voice has a great volume * the volume of a bottle

20 **suppose** The police supposed him to be a thief * Let us suppose the information is correct NOTE: Supposing it rains, what shall we do then? *(angenommen, es regnet)*

21 **thought** She scarcely favoured the thought of marrying him * I had no thought of hurting you *(hatte nicht die Absicht)*

22 **envy** I have always envied her ability to write letters * I don't envy his wealth *(beneide ihn nicht um seinen Reichtum)* ADJ: envious *(neidisch)*

23 **torture** It was a torture to hear him play the violin * He died under torture * She was tortured by the thought of losing him *(gequält)*

rest	*Rest; Ruhe; ruhen*
decay [dɪ'keɪ]	*Verfall; verfallen* [1]
narrow	*schmal; knapp* [2]
sound	*gesund; vernünftig* [3]
valuable	*wertvoll*
to deprive s.o. of s.th.	*jemanden einer Sache berauben;* [4]
native	*Einheimischer;einheimisch* [5]
both	*beide* [6]
both ... and	*sowohl ... als auch* [7]
to defend	*verteidigen , schützen* [8]
favourable	*günstig* [9]
motion	*Bewegung; Antrag* [10]
quarrel ['kwɒrəl]	*streiten, zanken; Streit* [11]
property	*Eigentum; Grundstück* [12]
review	*Rückblick; Überblick; Kritik* [13]
account	*Bericht; Konto* [14]
steep	*steil*
to impress	*beeindrucken* [15]
concrete ['kɒŋkrɪ:t]	*Beton; konkret*
jealousy (of) ['dʒeləsɪ]	*Eifersucht (auf); Neid (auf)* [16]
steady	*stetig; fest* [17]
to crush	*zerquetschen ; ausdrücken; vernichten* [18]
attempt	*versuchen; Versuch* [19]
to explore	*erforschen ; untersuchen* [20]
scarce ['skeəs]	*selten; knapp* [21]
wealthy ['welθɪ]	*reich ; wohlhabend*
to pursue [pə'sju:]	*verfolgen* [22]
revenge	*Rache* [23]
to long (for)	*sich sehnen (nach)* [24]

1 **decay** a house may be in decay; one's power, teeth etc. may decay

2 **narrow** a narrow road * a narrow escape NOTE: narrow-minded *(engstirnig)* VERB: to narrow *(verengen, sich verengen)*

3 **sound** a sound constitution, business, argument etc. * She is sound in mind and body *(körperlich und seelisch gesund)*

4 **deprive** He was deprived of his employment NOUN: deprivation

5 **native** He is a native of Australia, Bristol etc. *(er stammt aus ...)* * a native plant, animal etc. NOTE: native language *(Muttersprache)* * native speaker *(jemand, der eine Sprache als Muttersprache spricht)*

6 **both** I want both cakes * Both of them are good * Take them both BUT: neither of the two *(keiner von beiden)*

7 **both and** He is both a mechanic and a gardener

8 **defend** We must defend our country against enemies * We must defend the weak from harm

9 **favourable** a favourable advice, report, wind etc.

10 **motion** The sea is constantly in motion *(= series of movements)* * They agreed to it on the motion of Sir Walter

11 **quarrel** They quarrelled all morning ADJ: quarrelsome *(streitsüchtig)*

12 **property** This car is my property * We invested our money in property

13 **review** one's life in review * a review of the political events of the year * His new book has had a favourable review

14 **account** a newspaper account * a bank account * She gave an account of her travels ALSO: Don't do that on my account *(meinetwegen)*

15 **impress** She was much impressed by his valuable stamp collection ADJ: impressive *(eindrucksvoll)*

16 **jealousy** ADJ: He was jealous of his friend's successful career

17 **steady** a steady improvement * a steady table VERB: to steady *(stabilisieren)*

18 **crush** to crush a parcel, a fruit etc.; to crush out the juice from a lemon; a crushing defeat *(vernichtende Niederlage)* BUT: crash *(Unfall etc.)*

19 **attempt** He was found guilty of attempted murder * She failed in her attempt to win the race BUT: experiment *(wissenschaftlicher Versuch)*

20 **explore** to explore a continent, the moon, a problem NOUN: exploration

21 **scarce** scarce supplies, food, money *(knapp),* a scarce book *(selten)*

22 **pursue** The police pursued the thief * He pursued his studies at a technical college NOUN: pursuit the pursuit of a criminal *(Verfolgung)* * the pursuit of happiness *(Streben nach Glück)*

23 **revenge** They took revenge on him for what he had done * revenge is sweet

24 **long** The children were longing for a big ice-cream * Most of them were longing to go home NOUN: longing * a longing for peace, sleep, happiness etc.

dull	['dʌl]	*trübe; schwerfällig; langweilig* [1]
to scratch		*(zer)kratzen*
mood		*Stimmung* [2]
to testify		*aussagen; bezeugen* [3]
shape		*Form; Gestalt* [4]
connection		*Zusammenhang; Verbindung;Anschluss* [5]
matter		*Sache; Angelegenheit* [6]
no matter		*ganz gleich, egal* [7]
savings		*Ersparnisse* [8]
grain		*Getreide; (Samen-)Korn* [9]
to attach (to)		*befestigen (an)* [10]
to decline		*ablehnen; abnehmen; verfallen* [11]
although (though)		*obgleich, obwohl* [12]
as though / as if		*als ob* [13]
to resign		*verzichten; zurücktreten* [14]
resignation		*Resignation; Rücktritt* [15]
humble	['hʌmbl]	*bescheiden; demütig* [16]
to beg		*bitten; betteln* [17]
beggar		*Bettler*
idle	['aɪdl]	*untätig; müßig; außer Betrieb* [18]
dust		*Staub* [19]
to refuse		*sich weigern; abschlagen*
screen		*Filmleinwand; (Wand- etc.)Schirm*
tight	[taɪt]	*dicht; fest; eng* [20]
clue	[klu:]	*Anhaltspunkt; Schlüssel*
duty		*Pflicht* [21]
to swallow	['swɒləʊ]	*schlucken; verschlucken* [22]
emergency		*Notfall*
audience	['ɔ:dɪəns]	*Publikum; Zuschauer*

1 **dull** dull weather; dull pupils; a dull speech

2 **mood** I'm not in the mood for singing songs ADJ: moody *(launisch)*

3 **testify** The witness testified against him * She testified under oath *(sagte unter Eid aus)*

4 **shape** in the shape of a star, a circle etc. * shoes in all shapes and sizes * The hat had lost its shape NOTE: She's in good shape *(gut in Form)*

5 **connection** There is no connection between the two events * Good connections can be very useful * I missed my connection to Leeds

6 **matter** He knew nothing about the matter * He was very strict in the matter of obedience *(was Gehorsam betraf)* NOTE: As a matter of fact I am not really interested *(tatsächlich)* VERB: That does not matter to me *(macht mir nichts aus)*

7 **no matter** He's lying, no matter what he says

8 **savings** He lost all his savings *(seine gesamten Ersparnisse)* * a savings account with a bank * a savings-bank

9 **grain** There was not a grain of truth in what he said

10 **attach** She attached a sticker to her car * He didn't attach any importance to this fact ALSO: She was deeply attached to her parents *(hing sehr an ihnen)*

11 **decline** She declined to marry him * The manager was worried by declining sales figures

12 **although** She often goes to the theatre, (al)though she doesn't earn much

13 **as though** She looked as if she had just awoken * It isn't as though they were dishonest *(nicht daß sie unehrlich wären)*

14 **resign** He resigned his job * The Minister resigned from the cabinet

15 **resignation** He accepted his failure with resignation * The minister handed in his resignation *(reichte seinen Rücktritt ein)*

16 **humble** a humble house, car, person etc.

17 **beg** He begged (for) money * She begged mercy *(bat um Gnade)* * I beg your pardon! *(Entschuldigung!)* I beg to differ! *(Da bin ich aber anderer Meinung!)*

18 **idle** People who can't find work must be idle * It's idle to expect advice from them * All the machines were idle ALSO: an idle person *(faul)*

19 **dust** NOTE: dustman *(Müllmann)*; dustcart *(Müllauto)* VERB: That bookcase hasn't been dusted for ages *(abgestaubt)*

20 **tight** a tight knot *(fester Knoten)* * These shoes are too tight ALSO: tight money *(knappes Geld)*

21 **duty** duty to others *(gegenüber)*; sense of duty *(Pflichtgefühl)* * He is on/off duty *(im Dienst / außer Dienst)*

22 **swallow** He swallowed his meal *(schlang hinunter)* * They swallowed it whole *(glaubten es sofort)* * His earnings were swallowed up by his wife's bills *(wurden aufgezehrt)*

firm		*Firma; fest; standfest* [1]
to behave		*sich benehmen; sich verhalten* [2]
behaviour		*Benehmen; Verhalten*
absence		*Abwesenheit; Fehlen* [3]
hardly		*kaum* [4]
sweat	[swet]	*Schweiß; schwitzen*
while		*Weile, Zeit* [5]
during		*während* [6]
race		*Rennen; Rasse* [7]
ever		*jemals, je* [8]
pressure	[ˈpreʃə]	*Druck* [9]
to join		*sich anschließen; zusammenfügen* [10]
joint		*gemeinsam; Gelenk* [11]
except	[ɪkˈsept]	*außer; abgesehen von* [12]
glorious		*glorreich; prächtig*
shortage		*Mangel, Knappheit* [13]
kindness		*Freundlichkeit; Güte*
to solve		*lösen* [14]
to remind (of)		*erinnern (an); mahnen* [15]
to remember		*sich erinnern* [16]
severe	[sɪˈvɪːə]	*streng, hart; heftig* [17]
polite (to)		*höflich (gegen)*
to believe		*glauben* [18]
quarter		*Viertel; Gegend* [19]
familiar		*vertraut* [20]
screw	[skruː]	*Schraube; schrauben*
prize	[praɪz]	*(Sieges-)Preis* [21]
price	[praɪs]	*Preis* [22]
to climb	[klaɪm]	*(er)steigen; klettern* [23]

1 **firm** firm steps, muscles, a firm faith, voice etc.

2 **behave** He behaved badly towards them NOUN: He is certainly not known for good behaviour

3 **absence** I won't decide that in his absence ALSO: There was an absence of experts *(Mangel an)*

4 **hardly** I could hardly walk * You can hardly expect me to listen to such nonsense * I have hardly ever seen him *(kaum jemals)*

5 **while** We'll go to the seaside for a while * I saw her a short while ago NOTE: I meet him once in a while *(gelegentlich)* * The film isn't worth while seeing *(lohnt nicht)*

6 **during** We had a lot of fun during our holidays (during = preposition) BUT: She was cooking while I was reading (while = conjunction)

7 **race** a horse-race * a race against time * the human race

8 **ever** have you ever been in London? * A good education is more important than ever

9 **pressure** pressure of the atmosphere, in a tyre * Some people can only work under pressure

10 **join** to join a club, the army etc. * The Channel Tunnel will join Britain to France

11 **joint** a joint effort *(gemeinsam)* * a finger joint ALSO: She sometimes smokes a joint or two *(Haschischzigarette)*

12 **except** Nobody knew except me * I didn't know anything of the programme, except that it would be boring VERB: I except you from my criticism *(schließe aus)* BUT: to expect *(erwarten)*!

13 **shortage** a shortage of food, money, equipment, good ideas etc. SYN: lack NOTE: We were short of petrol *(hatten zu wenig Benzin)*

14 **solve** to solve a problem, puzzle etc. NOUN: solution

15 **remind** He reminds me of his father * Did you remind him of the book he borrowed? NOUN: reminder *(Mahnung)*

16 **remember** I remember him *(Ich erinnere mich an ihn)* ALSO: Remember me to your parents *(Grüße deine Eltern von mir)*

17 **severe** a severe punishment, injury, competition, pain etc.

18 **believe** I believe what he says * He believes in God NOUN: She hadn't much belief in his abilities

19 **quarter** a quarter of a mile, an hour, a pint etc. * the Chinese quarter of San Francisco *(Chinesenviertel)* * They came from all quarters *(von überall her)*

20 **familiar** That name seems familiar to me * I'm not familiar with this part of the town

21 **prize** He won the first prize at the competition

22 **price** He sold his motor-cycle at a good price * The price of success is high * I won't do that at any price!

23 **climb** to climb a mountain, the stairs, a tree etc. * Prices have been climbing again recently NOTE: The 'b' in climb is never pronounced!

joy		*Freude*	[1]
to mend		*ausbessern, flicken*	[2]
seldom		*selten*	
doubt	[daut]	*Zweifel; bezweifeln*	[3]
to cut down		*fällen; niederschlagen; herabsetzen*	[4]
frame		*Rahmen; Gestell*	[5]
scale		*Maßstab; Skala*	[6]
to mention		*erwähnen*	[7]
journey	[ˈdʒɜːnɪ]	*Reise*	[8]
to advance		*vorrücken; steigen*	[9]
variety	[vəˈraɪetɪ]	*Vielfalt; Auswahl*	[10]
merchant	[ˈmɜːtʃənt]	*Händler*	[11]
growth	[grəʊθ]	*Wachstum; Wuchs*	[12]
to care (for/about)		*sorgen (für); sich kümmern (um)*	
careful		*sorgfältig; besorgt*	
careless		*leichtsinnig; nachlässig*	
to grow up		*heran- / aufwachsen*	[13]
labour		*Arbeit; Mühe; Arbeitskräfte*	[14]
mercy	[ˈmɜːsɪ]	*Gnade; Mitleid*	[15]
to threaten	[ˈθretn]	*drohen; bedrohen*	[16]
justice		*Gerechtigkeit*	[17]
to twist		*drehen; verflechten*	[18]
merry		*fröhlich, lustig*	[19]
gift		*Geschenk; Gabe*	[20]
to discover		*entdecken*	[21]
certain		*sicher; gewiss*	[22]
abroad	[əˈbrɔːd]	*im Ausland; ins Ausland*	[23]
tiny	[ˈtaɪnɪ]	*winzig*	
to flourish	[ˈflʌriʃ]	*gedeihen; erfolgreich sein*	[24]

1 **joy** He was a good friend in joy and sorrow * She jumped for joy

2 **mend** to mend a watch, a machine, shoes etc. * ALSO: That won't mend matters! *(Das macht die Sache auch nicht besser!)*

3 **doubt** She doubted the truth of his statement * There can be no doubt about it

4 **cut down** to cut down a tree, an enemy; to cut down prices * She was trying to cut down on cigarettes *(ihren Zigarettenkonsum zu reduzieren)*

5 **frame** the frame of a picture, a window, a pair of glasses

6 **scale** the decimal scale * a scale in inches * They sold the articles on a large scale *(in großem Umfang)*

7 **mention** NOTE: 'You have been very helpful' 'Don't mention it' *(Gern geschehen, keine Ursache)*

8 **journey** They made a journey round the world, through Europe etc. * The journey will take eight hours

9 **advance** civilisation advances, troops advance * The prices continued to advance NOTE: advanced courses of study *(Fortgeschrittenenkurse)*

10 **variety** a variety of reasons, pictures etc.; a variety in food

11 **merchant** NOTE: merchandise *(Ware, Waren)*

12 **growth** the growth of plants, the population, an economy; the full growth of an animal

13 **grow up** A friendship grew up between them * children grow up NOUN: a grown-up *(Erwachsener)*; plural: grown-ups

14 **labour** manual labour *(Handarbeit)* * unskilled labour *(ungelernte Arbeitskräfte)* VERB: The old man laboured up the stairs *(mühte sich die Treppe hinauf)*

15 **mercy** Have mercy on me! * They didn't show mercy to him

16 **threaten** danger threatens * They threatened the enemy * He threatened to punish him in case he was late

17 **justice** Everybody has the right to be treated with justice * a court of justice *(Gericht, Gerichtshof)* OPP: injustice

18 **twist** to twist the cap off a tube * twist strings into a rope * You are twisting my words! *(drehst mir die Worte im Mund herum)* * tongue-twister *(Zungenbrecher)*

19 **merry** a merry child, song, evening etc. Merry Christmas *(Fröhliche Weihnachten)* NOTE: merry-go-round *(Kinderkarussell)*

20 **gift** SYN: present BUT: poison *(Gift)*

21 **discover** to discover a new continent * I discovered that he was a liar NOUN: discovery BUT: to uncover *(aufdecken)*

22 **certain** I'm certain I met her before * He is certain to come *(Er kommt sicher)* * I don't know for certain *(weiß nicht genau)*

23 **abroad** He lives abroad * I like travelling abroad

24 **flourish** plants, children, companies, projects etc. flourish SYN: prosper

knot	[nɒt]	*Knoten*
vanity		*Eitelkeit* [1]
schedule	[ˈʃedjuːl]	*Tabelle; Verzeichnis; (Fahr)plan* [2]
to lack		*(er)mangeln; nicht haben* [3]
to survive	[seˈvaɪv]	*überleben* [4]
hatred (of)		*Hass (auf)*
to assemble		*zusammenbauen, -tragen; versammeln* [5]
to increase		*zunehmen; erhöhen; vergrößern* [6]
line		*Linie; Strecke; Reihe; Zeile* [7]
glad		*froh* [8]
to furnish		*möblieren; ausstatten* [9]
to perform		*ausführen; vollbringen; aufführen; vortragen* [10]
to justify	[ˈdʒʌstɪfaɪ]	*rechtfertigen* [11]
to sum up		*zusammenfassen*
to disappoint		*enttäuschen* [12]
to boast	[bəʊst]	*prahlen* [13]
opposite		*gegenüber; gegenteilig ;Gegenteil* [14]
to avoid		*vermeiden* [15]
permission		*Erlaubnis, Genehmigung* [16]
to accompany		*begleiten* [17]
influence		*Einfluss; beeinflussen* [18]
knock	[nɒk]	*Klopfen; Stoß; klopfen; stoßen* [19]
male		*männlich; Männer-; Mann*
female		*weiblich; Frauen-; Frau*
loan	[ləʊn]	*Darlehen*
to foster		*fördern; hegen* [20]
to immigrate/emigrate		*einwandern / auswandern*
to grant		*gewähren, bewilligen* [21]

1 **vanity** He didn't use a stick out of vanity ADJ: vain *(eitel)*

2 **schedule** a production schedule in a factory * The train arrived on schedule VERB: It is scheduled for 10 a.m. *(soll um 10 Uhr ankommen)*

3 **lack** He doesn't lack friends * He lacks the necessary courage NOTE: He couldn't make the journey for lack of money

4 **survive** Few people survived the accident * Although he was forgotten, his ideas survived NOUN: survival *(das Überleben)*

5 **assemble** to assemble the parts of a car * to assemble material, equipment, a collection * They assemble in church every Sunday NOUN: assembly

6 **increase** prices, difficulties increase, someone's salary, production increases NOUN: There is a steady increase in population OPP: decrease *(abnehmen, schwinden)*

7 **line** a line from A to B * a bus line, an airline * a long line of famous kings * the last line on this page VERB: The market place was lined with trees *(umsäumt von)*

8 **glad** Glad to see you! * I"m glad of your success * I feel glad about your recovery

9 **furnish** to furnish a room with furniture * to furnish a camp with supplies * to furnish information to someone

10 **perform** to perform a task, duty, miracle * to perform a play ALSO: The engine is performing well *(arbeitet gut)*

11 **justify** A lack of money doesn't justify stealing NOUN: justification *(Rechtfertigung)*

12 **disappoint** NOUN: To my great disappointment it was raining when I arrived

13 **boast** You needn't boast about your talents * He boasted of his success NOUN: The old church is the boast of the town *(Stolz)*

14 **opposite** the opposite side of the house * My taste is completely opposite to yours * Opposites attract one another

15 **avoid** to avoid an accident, someone's company etc. * I couldn't avoid talking to him

16 **permission** I gave him permission to use my telephone * He took the car without even asking permission *(ohne überhaupt um Erlaubnis zu bitten)* VERB: His condition doesn't permit his coming

17 **accompany** They'll accompany us on our journey * Beauty is sometimes accompanied by arrogance

18 **influence** He has a bad influence on her * He used his influence in favour of the man * Don't be influenced by him *(lass dich nicht beeinflussen)*

19 **knock** a knock at the door * a knock on one's head * She knocked a nail into the wall

20 **foster** to foster a development *(fördern)* * to foster an idea, a thought *(hegen)* ALSO: to foster a child *(in Pflege nehmen)* * foster parents *(Pflegeeltern)*

21 **grant** to grant permission, a favour, a request, an interview * They will grant him more money NOTE: to take something for granted *(als selbstverständlich nehmen)*

stage	*Bühne; Stadium* [1]
to regard (as)	*betrachten (als); schätzen; berücksichtigen* [2]
regard	*Rücksicht; Aufmerksamkeit* [3]
in/with regard to	*in /mit Bezug auf*
meaning	*Sinn, Bedeutung* [4]
apart	*entfernt; abseits* [5]
to bias ['baɪes]	*beeinflussen* [6]
exception	*Ausnahme* [7]
surplus (of) ['sɜːpləs]	*Überschuss (an)*
gain	*gewinnen, erlangen; Gewinn, Profit* [8]
to frown [fraun]	*die Stirn runzeln* [9]
disease	*Krankheit; (Krankheitsart)* [10]
shy [ʃaɪ]	*schüchtern*
touch [tʌtʃ]	*Berührung; berühren* [11]
various	*verschieden(artig)* [12]
accurate ['ækjərət]	*exakt, genau*
to invent	*erfinden* [13]
to reveal [rɪ'vɪːl]	*enthüllen; zeigen*
consequently	*folglich, deshalb* [14]
just	*gerecht; genau; gerade* [15]
threat [θret]	*Drohung* [16]
performance	*Aufführung; Leistung* [17]
essential	*wesentlich; notwendig; Hauptsache* [18]
to dispose of	*loswerden; verfügen über* [19]
face	*Gesicht; Oberfläche* [20]
conviction	*(feste) Überzeugung; Verurteilung*
to modify	*abändern*
novelty	*Neuheit* [21]

1 **stage** She went on the stage *(wurde Schauspielerin)* * The child has reached the talking stage *(lernt jetzt sprechen)*

2 **to regard** I regard this as wrong * She regarded the gift highly * He often regards my advice ALSO: This doesn't regard me at all *(betrifft mich gar nicht)*

3 **regard** He has no regard for others * More regard must be paid to public opinion * In/with regard to this matter I must say ... *(hinsichtlich)*

4 **meaning** the meaning of a word, gesture etc. VERB: These new regulations mean more work *(bedeuten)* * I didn't mean to hurt you *(hatte nicht die Absicht)* BUT: I think that's not true *(meine, glaube)*

5 **apart** They were standing miles apart * She preferred to hold herself apart ALSO: Apart from the reasons you mentioned there are others *(abgesehen von)*

6 **bias** Politicians try to bias the opinion of people * The jury were biased by the aggressive behaviour of the accused

7 **exception** There is always an exception from the rule

8 **gain** to gain experience, popularity, admission, a victory etc. * a gain in knowledge, weight etc. * gains from a business

9 **frown** He frowned at her silly remark

10 **disease** a chronic, mild, children's, an incurable disease * She suffered from a serious disease

11 **touch** I felt her touch my arm ALSO: I got in touch with his parents *(setzte mich in Verbindung)*

12 **various** He called me at various times for various reasons

13 **invent** to invent a machine, method, a story etc. NOUN: The steam engine was Watt's invention

14 **consequently** You are willing to take the consequences for your actions, consequently you are responsible for them SYN: therefore BUT: consistent *(konsequent)*

15 **just** a just person, sentence etc. * This is just what I said * I have just opened the window

16 **threat** He uttered severe threats against his rival * He is a threat to society * There is a threat of rain

17 **performance** He had tickets for the evening performance * He was not content with the performance of the motor-bike

18 **essential** Speaking a language is an essential part of learning it * Personal security is an essential of a happy life ADV: This is essentially true *(im Wesentlichen)*

19 **dispose of** Let's first dispose of all that rubbish *(loswerden)* * You can dispose of my car *(verfügen über)* NOUN: My tools are always at your disposal *(stehen dir zur Verfügung)*

20 **face** the face of a person * the face of a clock, banknote etc. ALSO: In the face of danger she never loses her head *(angesichts einer Gefahr)*

21 **novelty** Not long ago a digital watch was a novelty * They were impressed by the novelty of her idea

to face		*gegenüberstehen; trotzen*	[1]
level		*eben; waagerecht*	[2]
bar		*Stange; Barriere; Theke; Bar*	[3]
to match		*sich messen mit; zusammen passen*	[4]
opportunity		*Gelegenheit*	
means		*Mittel*	[5]
to suffer (from)		*leiden (an /unter)*	
by no means		*auf keinen Fall*	[6]
bias	['baɪes]	*Vorliebe; Vorurteil*	[7]
to oppose		*entgegentreten; bekämpfen*	[8]
to admire		*bewundern*	[9]
ill		*krank; schlimm; schlecht*	[10]
patience	['peɪʃns]	*Geduld; Ausdauer*	[11]
to bless		*segnen*	[12]
manner		*Art und Weise; Benehmen*	[13]
cause	[kɔːs]	*Ursache; Grund; Sache*	[14]
library	['laɪbrərɪ]	*Bücherei, Bibliothek*	
to deserve	[dɪ'sɜːv]	*verdienen*	[15]
proposal		*Vorschlag*	
to judge		*beurteilen*	[16]
choice		*Auswahl; Wahl*	[17]
visible		*sichtbar*	
to fade		*verblassen; verklingen*	[18]
evident		*offensichtlich*	[19]
gate		*Tor*	
diligent	['dɪlɪdʒənt]	*fleißig; emsig*	
available		*verfügbar*	[20]
figure		*Zahl; Gestalt; Figur*	[21]
equipment	[ɪ'kwɪpmənt]	*Ausrüstung; Einrichtung*	

1 **face** Who is that facing you? * They were facing many difficulties ALSO: You must face up to the fact that this was a failure *(damit fertigwerden, akzeptieren)*

2 **level** a level ground NOUN: 500 metres above sea level * She's on a higher level than he

3 **bar** a bar of metal, wood; a bar of chocolate * Poverty is often a bar to social success * a quick-lunch bar

4 **match** I can't match him at playing chess * He tried to match his strength with his father's * His tie didn't match his shirt

5 **means** All possible means were tried to persuade him * a means of transport * She succeeded by means of a clever trick *(mittels)*

6 **by no means** That was by no means satisfactory NOTE: You should see that play by all means *(auf jeden Fall)*

7 **bias** He has a bias towards hot countries * The article shows a bias against the government's policy

8 **oppose** to oppose a person, a proposal, a plan, someone's wishes NOUN: opposition

9 **admire** I really admire his skill * I admire him for his courage NOUN: We were full of admiration for her

10 **ill** an ill health; an ill omen, experience; an ill temper, advice * Don't speak ill of him

11 **patience** OPP: impatience *(Ungeduld)* ADJ: patient *(geduldig)* BUT: the patient *(der Patient)*

12 **bless** to bless a church, the worshippers * He was blessed with good health NOUN: The rain was a blessing for the farmers * The accident proved to be a blessing in disguise *(erwies sich letztlich als Segen)*

13 **manner** He did it in the usual manner * He's got no manners

14 **cause** He has given me no cause to complain * The policeman made common cause with the thieves VERB: What caused the tree to die?

15 **deserve** These people deserve our help * Not all people deserve what they earn for their work

16 **judge** I judged from his manner that he was drunk * Don't judge him by his living standard

17 **choice** He had no choice but to go * He was very careful in the choice of his friends * The shop offers a large choice of records

18 **fade** colours fade *(verblassen)*; sounds fade *(verklingen)* * The hope of rescuing the members of the expedition was fading

19 **evident** SYN: plain, clear * It was evident that he was wrong ADV: They had evidently lost their way SYN: obviously

20 **available** There were no tickets available * More jobs should be made available for women

21 **figure** an income of five figures *(fünfstellig)* * the figure of a man in the dark * These figures represent characters from Roman history NOTE: He's good at figures *(im Rechnen)*

to confess	*gestehen; bekennen*	[1]
present (at)	*anwesend (bei)*	[2]
citizen	*Bürger*	
to recognize	*(wieder)erkennen; anerkennen*	[3]
admission	*Eintritt; Zutritt*	[4]
to pretend	*vorgeben; heucheln*	[5]
even	*eben; gleich(mäßig); sogar*	[6]
to share (in)	*teilhaben (an); teilen*	[7]
advance	*Fortschritt*	[8]
to diminish	*vermindern*	
convenient [kən'viːnɪənt]	*passend, geeignet*	[9]
opinion	*Meinung*	[10]
to introduce	*einführen; vorstellen*	[11]
fence	*Zaun; Hindernis*	[12]
to convert [kən'vɜːt]	*umwandeln, verwandeln*	[13]
determination	*Entschlossenheit; Festlegung*	[14]
to recommend	*empfehlen*	
effort	*Anstrengung, Mühe*	
to invite	*einladen; auffordern*	
proper	*passend; richtig*	
to bring about	*zustandebringen*	
judge [dʒʌdʒ]	*Richter*	
civil	*bürgerlich; zivil*	[15]
successive [sʌk'sesɪv]	*aufeinanderfolgend*	[16]
to advertise	*werben; annoncieren*	[17]
foreign ['fɒrən]	*ausländisch; fremd*	[18]
to fail	*misslingen; fehlschlagen; versagen*	[19]
to accuse	*anklagen*	
mature [mə'tjʊə]	*reif; durchdacht*	[20]

1 **confess** She refused to confess * I have to confess it was my fault NOUN: He made a full confession *(ein volles Geständnis)*

2 **present** We were all present at the party BUT: We don't need you at present *(im Augenblick)*

3 **recognize** I recognized that I wasn't fit for the job * I didn't recognize him after such a long time * They recognized him as the leader of their team

4 **admission** ALSO: an apology is an admission of failure *(Eine Entschuldigung ist das Eingeständnis eines Fehlers)*

5 **pretend** She pretended not to know us *(tat, als ob sie uns nicht kannte)*

6 **even** an even table, even scores in a game, even breathing * Even a child can understand this * They didn't even ask *(fragten nicht einmal)* NOTE: even/odd numbers *(gerade/ungerade Zahlen)*

7 **share** to share money, a room, troubles, experiences etc.

8 **advance** an advance in technology * with advance of old age *(mit zunehmendem Alter)*

9 **convenient** a convenient date for a meeting * a convenient method

10 **opinion** What's your opinion on that? * in my opinion *(meiner Meinung nach)* * I'm of the opinion that this is wrong *(bin der Meinung)*

11 **introduce** to introduce new machines, a book in class etc. * She introduced me to her father NOUN: a speech of introduction

12 **fence** They fenced in their land *(zäunten ein)* VERB: to fence in *(einzäunen)*

13 **convert** The house was converted into two flats * He converted his euros into pounds *(tauschte um)*

14 **determination** a determination to do something * The exact determination of the meaning of certain words is very difficult

15 **civil** NOTE: civil disobedience *(passiver Widerstand)* * civil engineer *(Bauingenieur)* * civil service *(Staatsdienst)*

16 **successive** They won three successive games *(drei Spiele hintereinander)* NOUN: successor *(Nachfolger)* OPP: predecessor *(Vorgänger)*

17 **advertise** He advertised his old car in the newspaper (= wanted to sell it) * She advertised for a second-hand bike (= wanted to buy one)

18 **foreign** She speaks three foreign languages * Telling lies is absolutely foreign to him *(ist ihm völlig fremd)* NOUN: foreigner *(Fremder, Ausländer)*

19 **fail** Our plan failed ALSO: He failed to win the game *(schaffte es nicht)* * She failed the exam *(fiel durch)* * Don't fail to see that film *(versäume nicht!)* * The examiner failed the candidate *(ließ ihn/sie durchfallen)*

20 **mature** He is very mature for his age BUT: a ripe apple VERB: to mature *(reifen)* NOUN: maturity *(Reife)*

promise	[ˈprɒmis]	*versprechen; das Versprechen*	[1]
height	[haɪt]	*Höhe; Gipfel; Höhepunkt*	[2]
to mark		*kennzeichnen; benoten*	[3]
confidence		*Vertrauen*	[4]
ordinary		*gewöhnlich; alltäglich*	
to admit		*zugeben, eingestehen*	[5]
reward		*Belohnung*	
to claim		*beanspruchen; behaupten*	[6]
tongue	[tʌŋ]	*Zunge; Sprache*	[7]
not even		*nicht einmal*	
to depend (on)		*abhängen (von); sich verlassen (auf)*	[8]
share		*Anteil; Aktie*	[9]
compulsory	[kəmˈpʌlsərɪ]	*verpflichtend; Pflicht-*	[10]
to refer (to)	[rɪˈfɜː]	*verweisen(an/auf); sich beziehen(auf)*	11]
opinion poll		*Meinungsumfrage*	
to irritate		*reizen; ärgern*	[12]
coward		*Feigling*	
distinct (from)		*verschieden (von); deutlich*	[13]
gay	[geɪ]	*lustig, vergnügt; homosexuell*	
to fix		*befestigen; festlegen; fixieren*	[14]
shore		*Ufer; Küste*	[15]
tough	[tʌf]	*zäh; schwierig*	[16]
in advance		*im Voraus*	
to determine		*bestimmen; beschließen*	[17]
apprentice		*Lehrling*	
veil	[veɪl]	*Schleier; verschleiern*	
judgement		*Urteil*	[18]
still		*noch; trotzdem; still*	[19]
apparent		*offenbar, offensichtlich*	[20]

1 **promise** to make, keep, break a promise *(Ein Versprechen geben, halten, brechen)*

2 **height** the height of a mountain, tree, person etc. * the height of his stupidity *(der Gipfel seiner Dummheit)*

3 **mark** The important words were marked in red * The invention of the car marked the beginning of a new era * The teacher spent the afternoon marking the students' tests

4 **confidence** VERB: He confided his trouble to me *(vertraute an)* ADJ: He feels confident of solving the problem *(zuversichtlich, dass er das Problem lösen wird)*

5 **admit** ALSO: They were admitted to the school *(zugelassen)* * The hall admits only few people *(fasst nur wenige)* NOUN: admission free *(Eintritt frei)*

6 **claim** He claimed the piece of land for himself *(beanspruchte)* * She claimed to be the best dancer *(behauptete, sie sei)* NOUN: They laid claim to the land *(erhoben Anspruch auf das Land)*

7 **tongue** NOTE: to hold one's tongue *(den Mund halten)* * mother tongue *(Muttersprache)*

8 **depend** He depends on welfare *(lebt von der Wohlfahrt)* * Can I depend on this information? *(Kann ich mich auf diese Informationen verlassen)*

9 **share** to have a share in the expenses, profits etc. NOTE: share-holder *(Aktionär)*

10 **compulsory** compulsory military service *(Wehrpflicht)*, a compulsory subject at school *(Pflichtfach)* OPP: optional *(Wahl-)*, voluntary *(freiwillig)*

11 **refer** I was referred to the manager *(verwiesen an)* * That does not refer to me *(geht mich nichts an)* * He referred his excellent health to drinking lots of tea *(führte darauf zurück)*

12 **irritate** ADJ: irritable *(reizbar)* NOUN: irritation *(Reizung, Gereiztheit)*

13 **distinct** In his manners he is very distinct from his brother * There was a distinct smell of alcohol in the room NOUN: A distinction between the twins was almost impossible *(Unterscheidung)*

14 **fix** He fixed a shelf to the wall * She fixed the facts in her mind * They fixed the rent of the house * I fixed my eyes on her

15 **shore** a house on the shore * He went on shore/ashore *(an Land)*

16 **tough** a steak tough as leather, a tough fighter *(zäh)* * a tough problem *(schwierig)*

17 **determine** They determined the date of their marriage * They determined to go to Italy

18 **judgement** The judge passed judgement on him *(fällte das Urteil)* * He has good judgement *(Urteilsvermögen)*

19 **still** He still hasn't come *(noch nicht)* * Still, she is my friend *(trotzdem)* SYN: however * a still voice *(leise)*

20 **apparent** His motives soon became apparent ADV: Apparently she was not at home SYN: obviously, evidently

to waste	*verschwenden* [1]
to expand	*ausdehnen* [2]
pile	*Haufen; Stoß; Pfahl* [3]
to worry (about)	*sich sorgen (um)*
above [əˈbʌv]	*oben; über*
mark	*Marke, Zeichen; (Schul-)note*
chance	*Gelegenheit; Möglichkeit* [4]
demand	*Forderung; Bedarf; Nachfrage* [5]
to distinguish (from)	*unterscheiden (von)* [6]
addict [ˈædɪkt]	*(Drogen-) Abhängiger* [7]
to encourage/discourage	*ermutigen/ entmutigen* [8]
affluent	*wohlhabend, reich* [9]
even so	*trotzdem* [10]
precious [ˈpreʃəs]	*kostbar*
to cheat	*betrügen* [11]
measure [ˈmeʒə]	*Maß; Maßnahme* [12]
to lean (against)	*sich lehnen (an)* [13]
greed	*Gier* [14]
faith [feɪθ]	*Glaube* [15]
to advise	*(be)raten* [16]
square	*Viereck; Platz; quadratisch*
to contradict	*widersprechen* [17]
proof	*Beweis*
common	*gemeinsam; allgemein; gewöhnlich* [18]
to launch [lɔːntʃ]	*beginnen; starten* [19]
aware	*bewusst* [20]
order	*(An)Ordnung; (Reihen)Folge; Befehl*
pattern	*Muster* [21]
attitude	*Haltung; Verhalten; Einstellung* [22]

1 **waste** to waste energy, time, money, resources, words etc.

2 **expand** methods, trades etc. expand NOUN: the expansion of a territory, of gases etc.

3 **pile** a pile of books, newspapers etc. ALSO: We had piles of work to do SIMILAR: heap *(Haufen)*

4 **chance** ALSO: They left it to chance *(überließen es dem Zufall)* * They met by chance *(trafen sich zufällig)*

5 **demand** the workers' demand for higher incomes * There is little demand for teachers nowadays * There was a great demand for cold drinks VERB: This demands a quick reaction *(erfordert)*

6 **distinguish** Some people can't distinguish between good and bad * Can you distinguish a spruce from a fir? *(eine Fichte von einer Tanne)* ALSO: She distinguishes herself by her cleverness *(zeichnet sich aus)*

7 **addict** VERB: He is addicted to TV *(fernsehsüchtig)* * He is addicted to lying *(er kann gar nicht anders als lügen)*

8 **encourage** We encouraged him to try it again * Kids should be discouraged from smoking

9 **affluent** NOTE: affluent society *(Wohlstandsgesellschaft)* NOUN: affluence *(Reichtum, Überfluss)*

10 **even so** He's not very smart, even so I honour him SYN: still

11 **cheat** to cheat at cards *(beim Kartenspiel betrügen)* BUT: fraud *(Betrug)*

12 **measure** Her dress was made to measure *(nach Maß)* * A metre is a measure of length * They took measures against inflation *(ergriffen Maßnahmen)* VERB: It is difficult to measure the speed of an electron * The garden measures 40 square metres

13 **lean** to lean out of a window, backwards, upon one's elbows , a ladder against a tree, etc.

14 **greed** greed for money, possessions, food etc. ADJ: greedy

15 **faith** to have faith in God, in what someone says, etc. * the Christian faith

16 **advise** I advised him to stay * She advised him medical treatment *(riet ihm zu medizinischer Behandlung)* * He advised me against buying that car *(riet mir ab)*

17 **contradict** I contradicted him * I contradicted to his statement NOUN: contradiction *(Widerspruch)*

18 **common** They have a lot in common *(gemeinsam)* * a common mistake *(häufig anzutreffender Fehler)* * She doesn't mix with common people *(mit gewöhnlichen Leuten)* NOTE: common sense *(gesunder Menschenverstand)*

19 **launch** to launch a business, an attack, a campaign etc. * to launch a rocket, a missile, a spaceship * The shipping company launched a new tanker *(ließ vom Stapel)*

20 **aware** Are you aware of what you are saying? *(ist dir bewusst...)* * I was aware of the risks involved *(Ich war mir der damit verbundenen Risiken bewusst)* NOUN: awareness

21 **pattern** the pattern of a wallpaper, a pattern of events, a behaviour pattern BUT: sample *(Warenmuster, Probe)*

22 **attitude** I don't like their attitude towards work

to meet demands	*Ansprüche befriedigen*
lie [laɪ]	*Lüge; lügen* [1]
faint	*schwach; (in) Ohnmacht (fallen)*
blame	*Schuld; Tadel* [2]
to pile up	*aufhäufen* [3]
waste	*wüst; öde; Abfall; Verschwendung* [4]
harm	*Schaden; Unglück* [5]
to interfere [ˌɪntəˈfɪə]	*sich einmischen; stören* [6]
above all	*vor allem*
sentence	*Urteil; Satz* [7]
to consist (of)	*bestehen aus* [8]
toy	*Spielzeug*
to remove	*beseitigen, entfernen* [9]
degree	*Grad; Stufe; Rang* [10]
to pity	*bemitleiden* [11]
even though	*selbst wenn, wenn auch* [12]
brave	*tapfer; tüchtig* [13]
by chance	*zufällig* [14]
to consider	*erwägen; berücksichtigen; betrachten als* [15]
glue [gluː]	*Klebstoff* [16]
to desert [dɪˈzɜːt]	*im Stich lassen* [17]
lean	*mager* [18]
fragile [ˈfrædʒaɪl]	*zerbrechlich*
to please	*gefallen; erfreuen* [19]
faithful [ˈfeɪθfl]	*treu; gewissenhaft* [20]
arrangement	*Abmachung* [21]
confusion	*Verwirrung*
to rescue	*retten; erretten* [22]
obstacle	*Hindernis* [23]

1 **lie** He is telling lies * He lies to me BUT: The carpet lies on the floor *(liegt)*

2 **blame** She didn't know where the blame lay *(wo die Schuld lag)* * He is not to blame *(Ihn trifft keine Schuld)* ADJ: He felt entirely blameless *(schuldlos)*

3 **pile up** His work piled up before him *(stapelte sich)* NOTE: a pile-up *(Massenkarambolage)*

4 **waste** waste land NOTE: waste-paper-basket

5 **harm** Last night's thunderstorm did a lot of harm to the crop *(richtete großen Schaden an der Ernte an)* ADJ: harmful *(gefährlich, schädlich)* * harmless *(ungefährlich, unschuldig)*

6 **interfere** They interfered in the negotiations * I'm afraid this interferes with my plans ALSO: Don't interfere with me when I'm on the phone *(störe mich nicht)*

7 **sentence** The sentence was/he was sentenced to/one year imprisonment

8 **consist of** beer consists of water, hops and malt

9 **remove** to remove a cloth from the table, doubts about a problem

10 **degree** an angle of 40 degrees *(Winkel von 40 Grad)* * 10 degrees centigrade *(10 Grad Celsius)* * various degrees of skill *(unterschiedliche Geschicklichkeitsstufen)* * the degree of Bachelor of Arts *(akademischer Grad)*

11 **pity** NOTE: what a pity *(wie schade)*

12 **even though** SYN: even if * I'll go to the concert even if it costs a fortune * He won't answer the phone even though it's ringing all the time

13 **brave** VERB: The sailors braved the storm *(trotzten dem Sturm)*14 **by chance** I met her by chance the other day ALSO: I happened to meet her the other day SYN: by accident

15 **consider** He is considering moving to Munich *(er erwägt)* * He is forgetful, but please consider his age *(berücksichtigen)* * He was considered fit for the job NOUN: The plans are under consideration *(werden überdacht)*

16 **glue** VERB: to glue *(kleben)* * They were glued to the TV set

17 **desert** to desert one's wife, a post in time of war ALSO: The streets were deserted *(verlassen, menschenleer)*

18 **lean** a lean person, harvest, income etc.

19 **please** The answer pleased him * I was pleased to meet him again

20 **faithful** a faithful friend, servant, dog etc. * a faithful copy *(eine genaue Kopie)*

21 **arrangement** ALSO: arrangement of furniture *(Anordnung, Verteilung)* * arrangement for a trip *(Vorbereitungen)*

22 **rescue** to rescue someone from fire, an attack, poverty, an embarrassing situation etc. NOUN: They came to her rescue

23 **obstacle** They stopped the car in front of the obstacle * His laziness proved an obstacle to his career

to prevent (from)		*abhalten (von)*	[1]
subject		*Thema; Untertan; Unterrichtsfach*	[2]
to attend		*besuchen; beiwohnen*	[3]
pretty	[ˈprɪtɪ]	*hübsch; ziemlich, beträchtlich*	[4]
to hesitate		*zögern, zaudern*	
border		*Grenze; Rand*	[5]
to strive (for, after)		*streben (nach)*	[6]
comfort	[ˈkʌmfət]	*Bequemlichkeit; Trost; trösten*	[7]
to occur	[əˈkɜː]	*sich ereignen; einfallen*	[8]
riot	[ˈraɪet]	*Aufruhr; Tumult*	[9]
to separate (from)		*trennen (von), absondern*	[10]
to arrange		*ordnen; einrichten; abmachen*	[11]
awful	[ˈɔːfl]	*schrecklich, furchtbar*	
to gather		*sammeln; sich ansammeln*	[12]
plain		*einfach; flach; Ebene; Fläche*	[13]
to bargain	[ˈbɑːgɪn]	*handeln; feilschen*	[14]
to compare (with)		*vergleichen (mit)*	[15]
defeat	[dɪˈfɪːt]	*Niederlage*	[16]
plant		*Pflanze; Fabrikanlage*	
to relieve		*erleichtern; befreien*	[17]
to engage		*anstellen; mieten; verpflichten*	[18]
brush	[brʌʃ]	*Bürste; Pinsel; bürsten*	[19]
famous (for)		*berühmt (wegen, für)*	
sufficient	[səˈfɪʃnt]	*ausreichend, genügend*	
weakness		*Schwäche*	[20]
to complain (of, about)		*klagen. sich beklagen (über)*	
obligation		*Verpflichtung*	[21]
fairly		*ziemlich*	[22]
burden	[ˈbɜːdn]	*Last*	[23]

1 **prevent** to prevent an accident, a disaster, an action etc. * They prevented him (from) committing a crime

2 **subject** They had long talks on the subject of pollution * English, Scottish and Welsh people are all British subjects * Chemistry is his favourite subject

3 **attend** to attend school, a meeting etc. ALSO: You should attend to what he says *(aufpassen auf)*

4 **pretty** She did pretty well in the test *(machte es recht gut)*

5 **border** the border between two countries; the border of a lake VERB: France borders on Germany * What he has said borders on impertinence *(grenzt an Unverschämtheit)* BUT: the limit of his financial means

6 **strive** ALSO: to strive against *(ankämpfen gegen)*

7 **comfort** His words comforted her for her misfortune

8 **occur** The accident occurred early in the morning * It didn't occur to him to help me *(fiel ihm nicht ein)*

9 **riot** VERB: They were rioting in the street *(randalierten)*

10 **separate** He can't separate fact from fiction * The garden was separated from the street by a fence * Late in the evening they separated *(trennten sich)*

11 **arrange** ALSO: I wasn't able to arrange their dispute *(schlichten)* SYN: settle

12 **gather** to gather information, speed, flowers etc. NOUN: gathering *(Treffen)*

13 **plain** a policeman in plain clothes *(in Zivil)* * the plain truth *(die reine Wahrheit)*

14 **bargain** They bargained over the price

15 **compare** NOUN: comparison *(Vergleich)* * In comparison with yesterday the weather has improved ADV: comparatively *(vergleichsweise)*

16 **defeat** NOTE: to suffer defeat *(eine Niederlage erleiden)* VERB: they defeated the other team *(besiegten)*

17 **relieve** I was relieved to hear that he was well again * I relieved him of his heavy bag

18 **engage** We engaged her as a guide *(engagierten sie)* * ALSO: an engaging smile *(gewinnendes Lächeln)* BUT: a committed environmentalist *(ein engagierter Umweltschützer)* NOTE: He can't come tomorrow, he is otherwise engaged *(beschäftigt)* * That number is engaged *(der Telefonanschluss ist besetzt)*

19 **brush** NOTE: to brush up *(auffrischen)* * My French isn't as good as it used to be, it needs brushing up

20 **weakness** ALSO: He has a weakness for ice-cream

21 **obligation** VERB: She was obliged to close the shop *(gezwungen)*

22 **fairly** SYN: rather, quite It was a fairly difficult problem

23 **burden** Being very strong, he could carry the heavy burden easily * a large tax burden *(Steuerlast)* BUT: a heavy load *(Ladung)*

season	*Jahreszeit; Saison* [1]
to disguise [dɪsˈgaɪz]	*sich verkleiden; verstellen* [2]
aim (at)	*Ziel; Zweck; zielen (auf)* [3]
virtue [ˈvɜːtʃuː]	*Tugend* [4]
substitute	*Ersatz; ersetzen* [5]
residence	*Wohnsitz; vornehmes Wohnhaus* [6]
to be pleased with	*sich freuen über*
to confuse	*verwirren; verwechseln* [7]
iron [ˈaɪen]	*Eisen; Bügeleisen; bügeln* [8]
length	*Länge* [9]
plenty (of)	*Fülle; Überfluss (an)*
to settle	*besiedeln; sich niederlassen; (Streit) schlichten* [10]
trace	*Spur* [11]
to conceive [kənˈsɪːv]	*ausdenken; ersinnen* [12]
inventive	*erfinderisch*
to suggest	*vorschlagen; zu bedenken geben* [13]
to cease [sɪːs]	*aufhören* [14]
wire	*Draht; Telegramm* [15]
independent (of)	*unabhängig (von)* [16]
arrival	*Ankunft* [17]
bargain [ˈbɑːgɪn]	*(Gelegenheits-)Kauf; Geschäft* [18]
sight	*Anblick; Sehenswürdigkeit* [19]
to trust (in)	*sich verlassen (auf); vertrauen*
display	*(Schaufenster-)Auslage; zeigen; zur Schau stellen* [20]
to imagine	*sich vorstellen; sich einbilden*
sick	*krank; unwohl* [21]
craft [krɑːft]	*Handwerk; Geschicklichkeit*

1 **season** the four seasons: spring, summer, autumn/fall, winter * the football season, the hunting season etc. * season-ticket *(Dauerkarte)*

2 **disguise** He disguised himself as a clown * She disguised her voice * He couldn't disguise his feelings *(verbergen)*

3 **aim** to aim with a gun at a target * His aim was to win the race * What are you aiming at? *(Worauf willst du hinaus?)*

4 **virtue** ADJ: virtual *(wirklich, tatsächlich)* * He owned the shop but the virtual boss was his wife

5 **substitute** A hot dog is a poor substitute for a real meal *(ein schlechter Ersatz)* * to substitute silver for gold *(Gold durch Silber ersetzen)*

6 **residence** NOTE: resident *(Bewohner, Anwohner)* * For residents only *(Nur für Anwohner!)* VERB: They resided in a manor house *(bewohnten ein Herrenhaus)*

7 **confuse** I was confused by all that noise * Don't confuse the words soap and soup! * The heavy rain confused the times of departure *(brachte die Abfahrtszeiten durcheinander)*

8 **iron** ADJ: an iron gate *(eisernes Tor)* * She had an iron constitution * This shirt badly needs ironing

9 **length** NOTE: at length *(schließlich, endlich)* SYN: in the end

10 **settle** They were the first who settled the country * Snow was settling on the tree * It was not easy to settle the dispute

11 **trace** VERB: The police were unable to trace the thief *(konnte ihn nicht aufspüren/ausfindig machen)*

12 **conceive** Daimler and Benz conceived the idea of a self-propelled vehicle *(ersannen)* ALSO: I conceived that he had misunderstood me *(begriff)*

13 **suggest** I suggested a trip to the seaside * The movement of his hands suggested impatience *(deutete an/zeigte)* NOUN: suggestion *(Vorschlag)*

14 **cease** At length they ceased to fight * This shop has ceased to exist NOTE: cease-fire *(Waffen-stillstand)*

15 **wire** VERB: He wired me that he would come on Thursday *(telegrafierte)* NOTE: I heard it on the wireless *(im Radio)*

16 **independent** NOUN: independence *(Unabhängigkeit)* NOTE: Independence Day *(Amerikanischer Nationalfeiertag am 4.Juli)*

17 **arrival** NOTE: on my arrival *(bei meiner Ankunft)*

18 **bargain** NOTE: collective bargaining *(Tarifverhandlungen)*

19 **sight** The ship remained in sight for half an hour * He couldn't bear the sight of her ALSO: He lost his sight in the war *(verlor seine Sehkraft/ wurde blind)*

20 **display** Lots of bargains were on display in the shop-window SIMILAR: exhibition, show NOTE: fashion-display *(Moden-schau)*

21 **sick** he fell sick *(er wurde krank)* NOTE: seasick *(seekrank)*, homesick *(krank vor Heimweh)* ALSO: I'm sick of being called a coward *(habe die Nase voll davon, ein Feigling genannt zu werden)*

curious	['kjʊərɪəs]	*neugierig; sonderbar*	[1]
relief		*Hilfe; Erleichterung*	[2]
whereas	[wer'æs]	*wohingegen, während*	[3]
to possess		*besitzen*	[4]
complaint		*Beschwerde, Klage*	[5]
range		*Bereich; Auswahl*	[6]
to disturb		*stören*	[7]
size		*Größe; Format*	[8]
capital		*Hauptstadt; Kapital*	[9]
average	['ævərɪdʒ]	*Durchschnitt*	[10]
source	[sɔ :s]	*Quelle, Ursprung*	[11]
to require		*bedürfen; verlangen, fordern*	[12]
according to		*entsprechend, gemäß*	[13]
brain		*Gehirn*	[14]
to convince (of)		*überzeugen (von)*	[15]
stroke		*Schlag, Hieb; Stoß*	[16]
pleasure		*Vergnügen*	
engaged		*beschäftigt; belegt; verlobt*	[17]
to maintain		*(aufrechterhalten); behaupten*	[18]
immediate		*unmittelbar; sofortig*	[19]
settlement		*Ansiedlung; Schlichtung*	[20]
frequent	['frɪ:kwənt]	*häufig*	
to trace		*ausfindig machen*	[21]
destruction		*Zerstörung, Vernichtung*	[22]
struggle (for/against)		*Kampf; kämpfen (um/gegen)*	
trust		*Vertrauen; Firmenzusammenschluss*	
to include		*enthalten, einschließen*	
to amount to		*sich belaufen auf, betragen*	[23]
access	['ækses]	*Zugang*	[24]

1 **curious** I'm curious to meet him * She was curious about his family * He made a curious remark SYN: strange, odd

2 **relief** To my great relief he was only slightly injured * Relief was sent to the victims of the disaster

3 **whereas** I enjoyed the voyage very much, whereas my brother got terribly seasick

4 **possess** He possesses two cars SYN: to own * She possesses many talents

5 **complaint** He made a complaint to the manager *(beschwerte sich bei)* * There is no cause of complaint *(kein Grund zur Beschwerde)*

6 **range** at a range of three miles *(im Bereich von)* * a range of colours, prices, interests etc. VERB: Their age ranges from 13 to 19 *(liegt zwischen 13 und 19)*

7 **disturb** to disturb the peace, one's sleep, one's order etc. * The thought disturbed him *(beunruhigte)*

8 **size** the size of buildings, shoes, gloves etc. * My shoes are size nine

9 **capital** ALSO: capital letter *(Großbuchstabe)* * capital punishment *(Todesstrafe)* * a capital mistake *(schwerwiegend)*

10 **average** on the average *(im Durchschnitt)* ADJ: average intelligence *(durchschnittliche Intelligenz)*

11 **source** the source of the River Thames * the source of an information, an income etc.

12 **require** They require our help *(bedürfen unserer Hilfe)* * What did he require of you? *(was verlangte/wollte er von dir?)*

13 **according to** according to plan *(nach Plan)* VERB: What he said didn't accord with my information *(stimmte nicht überein)*

14 **brain** NOTE: He used his brains *(gebrauchte seinen Verstand)*

15 **convince** I'm convinced that he can do it * I'm convinced of her honesty

16 **stroke** a stroke of a hammer, sword, a swimmer etc.

17 **engaged** She is engaged in business * The number is engaged (telephone) * They announced /that they were engaged /their engagement

18 **maintain** to maintain law and order * They maintained a good relationship * She maintained that she hadn't done it NOUN: maintenance *(Wartung eines Geräts)*

19 **immediate** an immediate contact, reaction, neighbour etc. * He came immediately SYN: at once

20 **settlement** the first English settlements in America ALSO; the settlement of a dispute *(Schlichtung, Beilegung)*

21 **trace** The police were unable to trace the suspect NOTE: He can trace his ancestors back to William the Conqueror *(zurückverfolgen)*

22 **destruction** the destruction of a town, a building, a person etc

23 **amount to** The bill amounted to five pounds

24 **access** the access to a building, a place, a person, information etc. * Only a few people had access to the staff-manager

general		*allgemein*	
fright	[fraɪt]	*Schrecken*	
skill		*Geschicklichkeit; Fertigkeit*	
imagination		*Vorstellungskraft; Fantasie*	[1]
curiosity		*Neugier*	
trade		*Handel; Geschäft; Handwerk*	[2]
weapon	[ˈwepən]	*Waffe*	
possession		*Besitz*	
rank		*Rang; Reihe*	[3]
a wide range of		*eine große Auswahl an*	
to prefer	[prɪˈfɜː]	*vorziehen*	[4]
impact		*Zusammenprall; Einwirkung*	[5]
entire		*ganz, vollständig*	[6]
to contribute (to)		*beitragen (zu)*	[7]
weight	[weɪt]	*Gewicht; Bedeutung*	[8]
to astonish		*erstaunen*	[9]
requirement		*Erfordernis; Anforderung*	[10]
entrance		*Eingang; Eintritt*	[11]
fair		*fair; angemessen; blond*	[12]
preference	[ˈprefrəns]	*Vorzug; Vorliebe*	
content	[kənˈtent]	*zufrieden*	[13]
to reach (for)		*greifen (nach); erreichen; sich erstrecken*	[14]
to spare		*verschonen; ersparen; erübrigen*	[15]
wet		*nass; feucht*	[16]
to establish		*gründen, errichten*	[17]
proof (against)		*sicher; geschützt (gegen)*	[18]
to hire		*mieten; anstellen*	[19]
to shift		*(weg)schieben; verlagern*	[20]

1 **imagination** Writing a novel requires a lot of imagination * I thought I had heard a noise outside, but it turned out to be only imagination *(nur Einbildung)*

2 **trade** NOTE: trade-mark *(Warenzeichen)* * trade agreement (Handelsabkommen) * trade-union *(Gewerkschaft)*

3 **rank** He was promoted to the rank of captain *(wurde zum Hauptmann befördert)* * a rank of taxis *(Reihe)* * taxirank *(Taxistand)*

4 **prefer** He preferred to stay at home * I prefer coffee to tea * She prefers reading a book to watching television

5 **impact** When the two planes collided most passengers died on impact *(im Augenblick des Zusammenstoßes)* * The nuclear disaster had a considerable impact on public opinion *(Wirkung)*

6 **entire** SYN: complete, total, whole

7 **contribute** to contribute money, ideas etc. * to contribute to charities, to one's ruin, success etc.

8 **weight** the weight of a stone, a person, a statement etc. * His opinion carries great weight VERB: to weigh *(wiegen; abwägen)*

9 **astonish** SYN: to surprise NOUN: astonishment *(das Erstaunen)*

10 **requirement** He couldn't meet his employer's requirements *(seine Anforderungen erfüllen)*

11 **entrance** NOTE: entrance examination *(Aufnahmeprüfung)* * entrance fee *(Eintrittsgeld / Aufnahmegebühr)*

12 **fair** He was given a fair trial *(ein fairer Prozess)* * She wanted a fair price for her painting *(einen angemessenen Preis)* * a fair-haired person ALSO: She has a fair chance of winning the race *(gute Aussichten)*

13 **content** She was quite content with her fortune *(ganz zufrieden mit ihrem Schicksal)* BUT: the contents of a case, book, letter etc. *(Inhalt)*

14 **reach** He often reached for that old book *(er griff oft nach)* * to reach a train, the end of something etc. * My land reaches as far as those trees

15 **spare** She spared his life *(verschonte sein Leben)* * I couldn't spare him the shock *(ersparen)* * He had no money to spare *(konnte kein Geld erübrigen)* BUT: to save money, time etc. *(sparen)*

16 **wet** wet road, clothes, eyes etc. NOTE: wet paint *(frisch gestrichen)*

17 **establish** The firm was established in 1865 * When I was a child it was an established custom to go to church on Sunday mornings

18 **proof** These windows are proof against housebreaking * foolproof *(narrensicher)* * waterproof *(wasserdicht)*

19 **hire** to hire a horse, a boat, a servant etc. * to hire a concert-hall BUT: to rent a house

20 **shift** to shift a heavy box; to shift the blame (on) to someone *(jemandem die Schuld zuschieben)* NOUN: shift *(Veränderung, Wechsel)* NOTE: shift work/ night shift *(Schichtarbeit / Nachtschicht)*

trouble	['trʌbl]	*Schwierigkeit; Unruhe*	[1]
to approve of		*etwas billigen*	[2]
to expect (of, from)		*erwarten (von)*	[3]
current		*Strömung; Strom; laufend*	[4]
to deceive	[dɪ'sɪ:v]	*täuschen; betrügen*	
urban	['ɜ:bən]	*städtisch; Stadt-*	
amount		*Betrag*	[5]
to frighten		*erschrecken*	
skilled worker		*gelernter Arbeiter*	[6]
carriage	['kæridʒ]	*Transport, Beförderung; Wagen*	[7]
to prove		*beweisen*	[8]
fortune	['fɔ:tʃn]	*Schicksal; Vermögen; Glück*	[9]
mere	[mɪ:ə]	*rein; bloß*	[10]
treasure	['treʒə]	*Schatz*	[11]
to whisper		*flüstern*	
delight		*Vergnügen; Entzücken*	[12]
prejudice	['predʒədis]	*Vorurteil*	
reasonable		*vernünftig; angemessen*	[13]
bold		*kühn; dreist*	[14]
spirit		*Geist; Stimmung; Gespenst*	[15]
expression		*Ausdruck; Redensart*	
appointment		*Ernennung; Verabredung*	
to deliver		*liefern; übergeben*	[16]
curse	[kɜ:s]	*Fluch; verfluchen*	
fair		*Messe; Jahrmarkt*	
to receive	[ri'sɪ:v]	*empfangen, erhalten*	[17]
to accustom (to)		*gewöhnen (an)*	[18]
spare time		*Freizeit*	[19]
to exploit		*ausnutzen; ausbeuten*	[20]

1 **trouble** The trouble is that she is too young *(Schwierigkeit)* * She has enough troubles *(Sorgen)* * a troublemaker *(Unruhestifter)* VERB: Don't trouble about it *(mach dir keine Sorgen)*

2 **approve** I've never approved of such behaviour * She didn't approve of his friend OPP: to disapprove *(missbilligen)* NOUN: He gave his approval *(Zustimmung)*

3 **expect** I expected their visit last week / too much of them / an answer of him NOUN: expectation *(Erwartung)*

4 **current** a current of air * the currents in the Atlantic Ocean * current money *(im Umlauf befindliches Geld)* * a current opinion *(allgemein verbreitete Meinung)* * current expenses *(laufende Ausgaben)*

5 **amount** an amount of money *(Betrag)* * quite an amount of interest *(eine ganze Menge)*

6 **skilled worker** NOTE: unskilled worker *(ungelernter Arbeiter / Hilfsarbeiter)* ADJ: skilful *(geschickt)*

7 **carriage** The carriage of goods by air is rather expensive * The train had only first class carriages

8 **prove** The accused failed to prove his innocence ALSO: The machine proved to be of no use *(stellte sich als nutzlos heraus)*

9 **fortune** It was his good fortune to find a loving wife * An astrologer told me my fortune * to make a fortune *(sich ein Vermögen erwerben)* ADV: fortunately *(glücklicherweise)*

10 **mere** I merely asked him to help me *(bat ihn lediglich)* * It wasn't a mere pleasure *(kein reines Vergnügen)*

11 **treasure** VERB: I treasure my father's advice *(schätze ihn sehr)* NOTE: treasurer *(Schatzmeister)*

12 **delight** He takes great delight in reading Shakespeare *(hat große Freude daran)* ADJ: delightful *(entzückend)* VERB: I was delighted to see them again *(freute mich sehr)* * He delighted a large audience with his play *(erfreute)*

13 **reasonable** a reasonable price, child, demand, suggestion etc. NOUN: You don't have any reason to complain *(Grund)*

14 **bold** NOTE: bold letters *(fettgedruckte Buchstaben)* BUT: bald *(kahl, kahlköpfig)*

15 **spirit** They were in high spirits *(guter Laune)* * The spirit is willing but the flesh is weak

16 **deliver** to deliver goods, a message, results etc. * to deliver a speech *(eine Rede halten)* NOTE: to be delivered of a child *(ein Kind gebären)*

17 **receive** NOUN: reception *(Empfang, Aufnahme)* * receiver *(Empfänger; Empfangsgerät))*

18 **accustom** She became accustomed to English meals *(gewöhnte sich daran)* SYN: to get used to

19 **spare time** SYN: free time, leisure NOTE: spare wheel *(Reserverad)*, spare part *(Ersatzteil)*, spare room *(zusätzliches Zimmer)*

20 **exploit** to exploit workers, an oil field, the generosity of other people etc.

conscience ['kɒnʃəns]	*Gewissen* [1]
to provide (for)	*sorgen (für); versorgen*
to distribute (among)	*verteilen (unter)* [2]
splendid	*glänzend; prächtig* [3]
recent	*jüngst; kürzlich* [4]
custom / customs	*Gewohnheit; Brauch / Zoll* [5]
to decide	*entscheiden; sich entschließen* [6]
beneath [bɪ'nɪːθ]	*unter; unten* [7]
expense	*Ausgabe; Kosten* [8]
to acquaint with	*bekanntmachen mit* [9]
to charge [tʃɑːdʒ]	*fordern, verlangen; belasten* [10]
to sigh (at/for)	*seufzen (über/nach)* [11]
bunch	*Bündel; Strauß* [12]
pride	*Stolz* [13]
record	*Rekord; Aufzeichnung* [14]
generous ['dʒenərəs]	*freigebig, großzügig*
to conquer ['kɒŋkə]	*erobern; besiegen*
decision	*Entschluss; Entscheidung* [15]
preparation	*Vorbereitung; Zubereitung*
advertisement	*Werbung; Reklame*
to resist	*widerstehen* [16]
court [kɔːt]	*Hof; Gericht* [17]
stain	*Fleck; beflecken* [18]
to treat	*behandeln* [19]
to dare	*wagen* [20]
crowd	*(Menschen-)Menge; Gedränge*
straightforward	*aufrichtig; gerade* [21]
to condemn [kən'dem]	*verurteilen; missbilligen*

1 **conscience** a clear/guilty conscience *(ein gutes/schlechtes Gewissen)* ADJ: conscientious *(gewissenhaft)*

2 **distribute** He distributed the presents to the children / among the children SYN: to hand out * This particular gene is unevenly distributed among the population

3 **splendid** a splendid meal, idea, goal, garden etc.

4 **recent** a recent meeting *(ein Treffen, das vor kurzem stattfand)* * I met him only recently *(erst kürzlich)*

5 **custom** It is my custom to stay up late *(ich habe die Angewohnheit)* * There are different customs in different countries *(unterschiedliche Gebräuche/ Sitten)* * It took us one hour to pass the customs *(durch den Zoll zu gehen)* * We had to pay customs on the cigarettes

6 **decide** It is difficult to decide on this question *(diese Frage zu entscheiden)* * I can't decide between the two of them *(zwischen den beiden entscheiden)* * He decided to leave the country *(er entschloss sich)*

7 **beneath** SYN: under, below * These remarks are beneath notice *(nicht wert, sie zur Kenntnis zu nehmen)* * It was beneath her to give an answer *(unter ihrer Würde)*

8 **expense** They spared no expense *(Sie scheuten keine Kosten)* * He saved the child at the expense of his own life *(auf Kosten)*

9 **acquaint** She made herself acquainted with the situation *(machte sich vertraut mit)*

10 **charge** How much do you charge for that? *(verlangen Sie dafür?)* * He was charged with murder *(wurde des Mordes angeklagt)* NOTE: free of charge *(kostenlos)* * to charge a battery *(Batterie laden)*

11 **sigh** NOUN: She gave a deep sigh of relief *(Seufzer der Erleichterung)*

12 **bunch** a bunch of bananas, flowers, keys etc. ALSO: a bunch of criminals

13 **pride** He took great pride in his wife's beauty *(war sehr stolz auf die Schönheit seiner Frau)*

14 **record** a world record * historical records

15 **decision** We have to come to / reach / arrive at / a decision *(zu einer Entscheidung kommen)*

16 **resist** Although it was cold we couldn't resist going for a swim

17 **court** court of law *(Gerichtshof)* BUT: yard *(der Hof eines Gebäudes)* * farm *(Bauernhof)*

18 **stain** blood-stained *(blutbefleckt)* * stainless steel *(rostfreier Stahl)*

19 **treat** He treated her badly * The doctor treated the injured leg * The problem has been treated often enough now

20 **dare** How dare he say that *(Wie kann er es wagen)* * He didn't dare to do it *(er wagte nicht, es zu tun))*

21 **straightforward** Please give me a straightforward answer ALSO: The author uses straightforward language *(leicht verständlich)*

undertaking	*Unternehmen* [1]
cruel (to) / cruelty	*grausam (gegen)/ Grausamkeit*
to present [prɪ'sent]	*vorstellen; überreichen; schenken* [2]
flat	*flach; Wohnung; Reifenpanne* [3]
application	*Anwendung; Bewerbung* [4]
experience	*Erfahrung; Erlebnis* [5]
charity ['tʃærətɪ]	*Nächstenliebe; Wohltätigkeit* [6]
resistance (to)	*Widerstand (gegen)*
enemy	*Feind*
flock	*Herde; Schar* [7]
to extend	*ausdehnen, verlängern* [8]
cloth [klɒθ]	*Stoff; Tuch*
to appoint	*festsetzen; bestimmen; ernennen* [9]
deed	*Tat* [10]
to reckon	*(be)rechnen; schätzen; denken* [11]
slight	*schwach; klein; unbedeutend* [12]
incredible	*unglaublich*
trial ['traɪel]	*Prüfung; Prozess; Verhandlung* [13]
to spoil	*verderben; stören* [14]
to calculate	*(be)rechnen* [15]
anxious (about, for)	*besorgt (um); ängstlich* [16]
treatment	*Behandlung*
to prepare (for)	*vorbereiten (auf); zubereiten* [17]
to be fond of	*gern haben, lieb haben*
advice	*Rat* [18]
extent	*Ausmaß, Umfang, Größe*
chase [tʃeɪs]	*Verfolgung, Jagd; (nach) jagen*
to alter ['ɔːltə]	*ändern; (sich) verändern*
emphasis	*Nachdruck, Betonung*

1 **undertaking** SYN: task, enterprise VERB: to undertake *(unternehmen)* BUT: undertaker *(Leichenbestatter)*

2 **present** The theatre group presents its new play *(stellt vor, führt auf)* * The cigars were presented to him as a birthday present *(wurden überreicht)*

3 **flat** The landscape around Lincoln is rather flat * The surface of a desk is flat ALSO: The meal is flat *(geschmacklos)* * Their conversation was flat *(langweilig)*

4 **application** The application of a new patent helped to solve the problem *(Anwendung)* * You must send in an application form *(Bewerbungsformular)*

5 **experience** You can learn that by experience only * Yesterday I had a funny experience *(Erlebnis)* NOTE: Never use 'make' together with experience!: We have had an experience *(haben eine Erfahrung gemacht)*

6 **charity** She gave money to charities *(Wohlfahrtseinrichtungen)*

7 **flock** a flock of sheep *(Schafherde)* * The people came in flocks *(in Scharen)* VERB: They flocked round the guide *(versammelten sich um)*

8 **extend** to extend a wall, a visit, a credit etc. ALSO: He extended his arm *(streckte seinen Arm aus)*

9 **appoint** They appointed a time for the meeting *(setzten fest)* * He was appointed for the post *(wurde für den Posten bestimmt)* * They appointed him president *(ernannten ihn zum Präsidenten)*

10 **deed** He has done many good deeds in his life * It is deeds that count, not words! NOTE: That's good news indeed *(Das sind in der Tat gute Nachrichten)*

11 **reckon** He reckoned how much money they would get *(rechnete aus)* * I reckon on your honesty *(zähle auf deine Ehrlichkeit)* * They didn't reckon that it would rain *(sie rechneten nicht damit)* * I reckon we'll arrive soon *(schätze, denke)* * I reckoned him to be the best player *(hielt ihn für den besten Spieler)*

12 **slight** The child was slightly built *(schwach gebaut)* * There is a slight error in your essay *(kleiner Fehler)*

13 **trial** She gave him a trial *(versuchte es mit ihm)* * First we must take the machine on trial *(erproben)* * Did you attend the trial yesterday? *(den Prozess)*

14 **spoil** Never eat spoilt (spoiled) fruit *(verdorben)* * Our holidays were spoilt by his visit *(gestört)* * a spoilt child *(ein verzogenes Kind)*

15 **calculate** I calculated how much money we would need for our holiday *(rechnete aus)* * They calculated that they would arrive rather late *(rechneten damit)*

16 **anxious** He was anxious about his money ALSO: They were anxious to go *(wollten unbedingt gehen)*

17 **prepare** to prepare for a test *(sich vorbereiten)* * to prepare a meal *(zubereiten)*

18 **advice** You ought to take my advice *(meinen Rat befolgen)* NOTE: a piece of advice *(Ratschlag)*

to investigate	*untersuchen; erforschen*	[1]
remark	*Bemerkung; bemerken*	[2]
to propose	*vorschlagen*	[3]
ancient ['eɪnʃənt]	*alt; ehemalig*	[4]
to flow	*fließen; strömen*	
damage	*Schaden; beschädigen*	[5]
item	*Posten, Punkt*	[6]
to scatter	*verstreuen; sich zerstreuen*	[7]
blast	*Explosion*	
to fasten (to)	*befestigen (an)*	
profession	*Beruf; Stand*	[8]
on account of	*wegen*	
remarkable	*bemerkenswert*	
concern [kən'sɜːn]	*Sorge; Wichtigkeit; Konzern*	[9]
to smell (of)	*riechen (nach)*	[10]
fault [fɔːlt] / faulty	*Fehler; Schuld; fehlerhaft*	[11]
to progress [prə'gres]	*Fortschritte machen*	[12]
besides	*außerdem; außer*	[13]
anxiety [æŋ'zaɪetɪ]	*Angst; Besorgnis*	
gap	*Lücke*	[14]
to perceive	*wahrnehmen*	[15]
zero ['zɪəreʊ]	*Null*	[16]
final	*endgültig; letztlich*	[17]
extension	*Erweiterung; Ausdehnung*	[18]
punishment	*Strafe*	
soil	*(Erd-) Boden*	[19]
cautious ['kɔːʃes]	*vorsichtig*	[20]
to detest	*verabscheuen*	[21]
incident	*Ereignis, Vorfall*	[22]

1 **investigate** The police investigated the matter BUT: The doctor examined his patient NOUN: investigation * Federal Bureau of Investigation (FBI)

2 **remark** She made a few remarks on the weather * Did you remark his smile? * He remarked that he was ill *(bemerkte, sagte)*

3 **propose** She proposed taking a trip to London SYN: to suggest ALSO: He proposed to her *(machte ihr einen Heiratsantrag)*

4 **ancient** the ancient Romans * an ancient castle, custom etc.

5 **damage** The fire did great damage to the house *(richtete großen Schaden an)*

6 **item** The catalogue contains hundreds of items * There were many interesting items on the news yesterday

7 **scatter** The leaves scattered in the wind * The branches of the bank are scattered over the whole town

8 **profession** He runs a little shop although he is an architect by profession *(von Beruf)*

9 **concern** He was filled with concern *(voller Sorge)* * This is no concern of yours *(geht dich nichts an)*

10 **smell** The room smelled/smelt of cheese * Due to a heavy cold he couldn't smell NOUN: There was a smell of salt in the air

11 **fault** There was a fault in his calculations *(Fehler)* * She does not have any faults *(Fehler)* * It was my own fault that I missed the train *(Schuld)*

12 **progress** The recovery of the patient was progressing rapidly NOUN: progress * We didn't make any progress *(keine Fortschritte)* * The report was in progress *(war im Entstehen)*

13 **besides** I don't think she likes me; besides she's too old for me *(außerdem)* SYN: moreover * I was the only man at the meeting besides him *(außer)*

14 **gap** a gap in a conversation *(Pause)*, between viewpoints *(Unterschied)*, in a fence *(Lücke)*, etc.

15 **perceive** On account of the darkness they couldn't perceive what was going on outside NOUN: perception *(Wahrnehmung)*

16 **zero** three, two, one, zero * It was ten degrees below zero * Our hopes were at zero BUT: In the last soccer match their score was nil

17 **final** His decision was final *(endgültig)* * On the final day of the meeting there was a firework display *(am letzten Tag)* ADV: finally *(schließlich)* SYN: in the end

18 **extension** an extension of knowledge, holidays, buildings etc.

19 **soil** This plant doesn’t grow in sandy soil * She was born on Irish soil BUT: The apple fell to the ground *(fiel zu Boden)* * A carpet covered the floor *(Fußboden)*

20 **cautious** NOUN: caution * You must use caution on icy roads (vorsichtig sein)

21 **detest** He detests snakes * I detest him for his greed * She detests visiting her aunt

22 **incident** ADJ: incidental *(zufällig; nebensächlich)* ADV: incidentally *(übrigens; nebenbei gesagt)* NOTE: coincidence *(Zufall)*

to afford s.th.		*sich etwas leisten* [1]
previous	[ˈpriːviəs]	*vorhergehend; vorangehend*
indifferent		*gleichgültig* [2]
to some extent		*in gewissem Maß*
to utter	[ˈʌtə]	*äußern* [3]
menace	[ˈmenəs]	*(Be-)Drohung; (be)drohen* [4]
case		*Fall; Sache; Prozess; Behälter* [5]
inevitable		*unvermeidlich*
vacation		*Ferien; Urlaub* [6]
temptation		*Versuchung; Reiz* [7]
to abolish		*abschaffen*
smooth	[smuːð]	*glatt; sanft* [8]
initial	[ɪˈnɪʃl]	*anfänglich*
to compete	[kəmˈpiːt]	*konkurrieren* [9]
artificial	[ˌɑːtɪˈfɪʃl]	*künstlich*
despair		*Verzweiflung; verzweifeln* [10]
obvious		*offensichtlich* [11]
to bother	[ˈbɒðə]	*belästigen; beunruhigen* [12]
enterprise		*Unternehmen, Unternehmung* [13]
to adjust (to)		*anpassen (an); einstellen (auf)* [14]
twin		*Zwilling* [15]
to deny		*leugnen; verweigern* [16]
to promote		*fördern; befördern* [17]
survey	[ˈsɜːveɪ]	*Überblick;Gutachten;Untersuchung* [18]
dense		*dicht; dick* [19]
poverty		*Armut*
to involve		*verwickeln; in sich schließen* [20]
obsolete	[ˈɒbsəliːt]	*veraltet, überholt*
to adapt (to)		*(sich) anpassen (an)* [21]

1 **afford** He couldn't afford a big car * I couldn't afford to fail the test again

2 **indifferent** The other guests were indifferent to / towards his bad behaviour *(den anderen Gästen war sein Benehmen gleichgültig)*

3 **utter** He uttered a sigh * She didn't utter a single word

4 **menace** This development is a menace to economy *(eine Bedrohung für die Wirtschaft)* SYN: threat * He sat there, uttering menaces *(stieß Drohungen aus)*

5 **case** This is not the case *(ist nicht der Fall, ist nicht wahr)* * I'll do it in your case *(in deinem Fall)* * cigarette case *(Zigarettenetui)*, violin case *(Geigenkasten)*, suitcase *(Koffer)* etc.

6 **vacation** They were on vacation *(im Urlaub)*

7 **temptation** It was a strong temptation to them *(für sie)* VERB: to tempt *(in Versuchung führen)* BUT: They tasted the wine *(versuchten, probierten)*

8 **smooth** a smooth sea, skin, road etc. * The negotiations went smoothly

9 **compete** They competed with each other for the prize * He competed in the race *(nahm am Rennen teil)* NOUN: competition *(Wettbewerb, Konkurrenz)*

10 **despair** I despaired of his indifference *(verzweifelte an seiner Gleichgültigkeit)*

11 **obvious** This was an obvious error * This was obviously an error

12 **bother** He bothered her with silly questions * His bad financial situation bothered him * She didn't bother to answer the letter *(machte sich nicht die Mühe)*

13 **enterprise** The first landing on the moon was a dangerous enterprise * spirit of enterprise *(Unternehmungsgeist)*

14 **adjust** I needed some time to adjust myself to the new situation * He went to the garage to have the motor of his car adjusted *(um den Motor neu einstellen zu lassen)*

15 **twin** He closely resembles his twin brother * a twin-engined aeroplane *(Flugzeug mit zwei Motoren)* ALSO: twin town *(Partnerstadt)*

16 **deny** She denied reading the letter * He denied that he had met her * He was denied admittance *(Man verweigerte ihm den Zutritt)*

17 **promote** to promote the sales of a product, a friendship, the career of a young artist etc. * He was promoted captain *(wurde zum Hauptmann befördert)*

18 **survey** She worked out a survey on the subject * Recent surveys have shown an increasing crime rate BUT: poll *(Umfrage)*

19 **dense** a dense smoke, fog * a dense forest, crowd * Germany is a densely populated country

20 **involve** On his way home he was involved in an accident * The application of new technologies often involves incalculable risks *(unberechenbare Risiken)*

21 **adapt** The camera can be adapted for use under water * This play has been adapted for radio and television * The immigrants had to adapt to a new culture

PHRASES FOR ORAL INTERACTION

1. Giving an opinion
(Meinung äußern)

To be honest

Frankly

Frankly speaking
Offen gesagt

If you ask me

I think/believe

In my opinion

Personally speaking, I think
Ich persönlich glaube

2. Suggestions, advice, recommendations
(Vorschläge, Rat, Empfehlungen)

How about/what about...?
Wie wäre es mit... ?

Why don't you/we

Listen, ...

Would you not consider
Wäre es nicht zu überlegen

If I were you

We could always …
Wir könnten ja immer noch ...

Let's …
(Wollen wir einmal …)

I think you/we should

Why not

We could recommend

We need to consider

The main priority is

It would make more sense to …

You'd/we'd better
Es wäre besser wenn du/wir

Wouldn't it be better to …

We will need to make some changes
Wir werden einige Änderungen vornehmen müssen

3. Asking and challenging
(Fragen und Herausfordern)

How do you feel about …
Was denkst du über ...

What exactly are you trying to say?

Where are the facts?

Prove it!

What are you driving at?
Worauf willst du hinaus?

What do you think about...?
What are your/their motives for...

What should be done about it?

4. Interrupting
(Unterbrechen)

Pardon me for interrupting you, but
Entschuldige, dass ich dich unterbreche, aber

What are you talking about?

Fine, but I still don't see what you mean

Just a second, please

May I ask you to make this specific?
Könntest du das genauer erklären?

Excuse me, but it's not true when you say

Allow me to say this:
Lass mich folgendes sagen:

I bet you don't realize that …
Ich wette, du siehst nicht, dass ...

That's a matter of argument
Darüber lässt sich streiten

Let me think

That's just the point
Darum geht es ja gerade

That goes without saying
Das ist doch selbstverständlich

I beg your pardon
Wie bitte?

Make it short

5. Changing your mind *(Meinung ändern)*

I've come round to the idea
Ich finde jetzt auch

I've/we've changed my/our mind about
Ich/wir habe(n) meine/unsere Meinung geändert über

I think differently about it now

Maybe I was wrong to/when I
Vielleicht war es falsch zu/als ich

6. Agreement *(Zustimmung)*

How very true
Wie wahr

Agreed!
Einverstanden!

I quite/totally agree

I couldn't agree more
Ich stimme völlig zu

That's a good way of putting it
Das ist gut gesagt

That's what I think
Das glaube ich auch

That's a great idea

That's a good point

So do I/am I
Ich auch

Absolutely!

Yes, definitely.
Ja, ganz bestimmt

That's exactly how I see it
Genau so sehe ich das auch

It's certainly worth a try
Das ist sicher einen Versuch wert

7. Disagreement *(Ablehnung)*

I beg your pardon, but don't you find that
Entschuldige, aber glaubst du nicht, dass

You don't really think so, do you?
Das glaubst du nicht wirklich, oder?

I'm afraid I can't agree with you there
Da kann ich dir leider nicht zustimmen

You can't be serious!

That's not how I see it
So sehe ich das nicht

That's simply not true
Das stimmt einfach nicht

You're wrong
Das ist falsch / Du täuschst dich

I totally disagree (with you)
Da stimme ich überhaupt nicht zu / mit dir überein

By no means / Not at all / No way! Not in the least
Keineswegs / Auf keinen Fall

You must be joking
Das kann doch nicht dein Ernst sein!

That's out of the question
Das kommt nicht in Frage

Oh, come off it, never!
Hör auf, niemals!

Make others believe that
Mach das anderen weis

That's utter rubbish!
Volliger Blödsinn!

8. Doubt *(Zweifeln)*

Well, maybe
Ja, vielleicht

I'm not so sure about that
Ich bin mir da nicht so sicher

I doubt that / whether …

I have my doubts about that
Ich bezweifle / habe da meine Zweifel

I'm not convinced by that
Ich bin nicht davon überzeugt

Ich don't see how that would work
Ich sehe nicht, wie das gehen würde

I have my problems with what you're saying

I'd say it depends on ...
Ich würde sagen, das hängt von ... ab

I don't think it's as simple as that
Ich glaube nicht, dass es so einfach ist

Are you sure?

You must admit that …
Du must zugeben, dass ...

9. Expressing criticism *(Kritisieren)*

That's all very well but
Alles schön und gut, aber

I don't think you know/realize/have understood

I don't see how you can say that …
Ich verstehe nicht, dass du sagen kannst, dass ...

You have to convince me yet
Da must du mich erst noch überzeugen

You seem to have forgotten
Du scheinst vergessen zu haben

That wouldn't work in practice
Das würde in der Praxis nicht funktionieren

I think you are missing the point
Darum geht es nicht

I don't see your point
Ich verstehe nicht, was du meinst

It's (un)likely that
Es ist (un)wahrscheinlich, dass

It could mean that
Es könnte bedeuten, dass

Are you seriously suggesting that …
Schlägst du ernsthaft vor, dass …

You can't be serious
Das kann nicht dein Ernst sein

You're not listening to a word I'm saying!

Du hörst überhaupt nicht zu!

That's bound to fail
Das muss schiefgehen / kann nicht klappen

Rubbish!
Blödsinn!

10. Agreeing in part *(Teilweise Zustimmung)*

Yes, but you forgot to mention that ...
Ja, aber du hast vergessen zu sagen, dass

Yes, but there's also another aspect to consider
Ja, aber da muss man noch einen anderen Aspekt berücksichtigen

You may have a point, but
Da könntest du Recht haben, aber

You've got a point, but
Das stimmt schon, aber

I agree with you up to a point
In gewisser Weise stimme ich dir zu

In a way, yes!
In gewisser Weise, ja!

I see what you mean, but
Ich verstehe schon, was du meinst, aber

Basically it's a good idea, but
Im Grunde eine gute Idee, aber

11. Indifference *(Gleichgültigkeit)*

It's all the same to me
Da besteht für mich kein Unterschied

I couldn't care less
Das interessiert mich überhaupt nicht

So what!
Na und?

What of it?
Und wenn schon?

12. General phrases and idioms *(Allgemeine Redewendungen)*

According to my knowledge

Well, as far as I can see
Meines Wissens

As far as I'm concerned
Was mich angeht

If I'm not mistaken
Wenn ich mich nicht irre

It all depends on...
Es hängt alles ab von .../ kommt darauf an

Never mind
Macht nichts

No matter what/why...
Ganz gleich was/warum ...

Take it easy
Immer mit der Ruhe! Mal langsam!

You never know
Man kann nie wissen

It's up to you
Das liegt an dir

That's just the point
Darum geht es ja gerade

I must admit that...
Ich muss zugeben, dass ...

You can take my word for it
Verlass dich drauf

I know what I'm talking about
Ich weiß, wovon ich spreche

I'm dead certain
Todsicher

ÜBUNGSSÄTZE

Übersetzen Sie die folgenden Sätze ins Englische. Wenn Sie die jeweilige Seite des Arbeitswortschatzes sorgfältig durchgearbeitet haben, sollte Ihnen das nicht allzu schwer fallen. Gelegentlich werden in Klammern kleine Übersetzungshilfen angeboten. Die Lösungen zu diesem Arbeitsteil finden Sie ab Seite 112

Seite 4

1. Er wurde verlegen, als ich darauf bestand, die Besprechung seines neuen Buches zu lesen.
2. In den letzten paar Jahren hat er die schlechte Gewohnheit angenommen, grob zu seinen Freunden zu sein.
3. Sie drängten ihn vergeblich, ihnen seine florierende Firma zu verkaufen.

Seite 6

1. Die beiden Seiten verhandelten miteinander, um die Lage zu verbessern und um den Missbrauch *(misuse)* der Waffen zu einem Ende zu bringen.
2. Die Polizei setzte ihre Nachforschungen über *(into)* das traurige Schicksal des Jugendlichen fort.
3. Der Schüler las den Textabschnitt kurz durch und erkundigte sich dann nach einigen Wörtern.

Seite 8

1. Die feindlichen Mächte verbrachten mehr Zeit damit, sich zu streiten, als zu versuchen, das dringende Problem der Abrüstung anzupacken.
2. Trotz der Kälte genoss er es, auf der Bank in seinem Garten zu sitzen.
3. Meine Großmutter versucht sich vor dem Verlust ihres Geldes dadurch zu schützen, dass *(by+ing)* sie es in einer leeren Blechbüchse aufbewahrt.

Seite 10

1. Der Beamte, der die Bank ausgeraubt hatte, wurde für schuldig befunden und entlassen.
2. Nach einer gründlichen Untersuchung wiederholte der Arzt zweimal seinen Ratschlag und verschrieb *(prescribe)* ein Mittel gegen die Magenschmerzen.
3. Im Großen und Ganzen schien sie das Ergebnis der Wahl zu befriedigen.

Seite 12

1. Sie berichtete, dass in einer der Vorstädte gerade eine neue Unterführung gebaut wurde.
2. Dem neuen Gesetz gemäß musste jeder Beamte über die Einzelheiten seiner Arbeit Bericht erstatten.
3. Es war die Aufgabe der Diener, die Miete und die Trinkgelder einzusammeln.

Seite 14

1. Ich bedauere es besonders bekanntzugeben, dass der jährliche Gewinn beträchtlich gesunken *(fall)* ist.

2. Ich wünschte dem gutaussehenden jungen Mann Zufriedenheit, Glück und große Leistungen bei *(in)* seiner Arbeit.
3. Mittlerweile hatten sie das Zelt aufgeschlagen *(set up)*, während ich gedankenverloren auf einem Kissen saß.

Seite 16

1. Ich war voller Bewunderung, als ich hörte, daß der Führer der Gewerkschaft den Mut gehabt hatte, die notwendigen Schritte einzuleiten *(take)*.
2. Bitte zieh dieses Hemd mit dem schmutzigen Kragen aus.
3. Ich konnte ihn nicht dazu überreden, mit dem Rauchen aufzuhören.

Seite 18

1. Die Diebe öffneten die Tür mit dem gestohlenen Schlüssel und stopften ihre Taschen mit allen möglichen Dingen voll.
2. Der Besitzer gab dem Kunden die Schuld an dem Schaden, und er wurde ersucht, das Geschäft zu verlassen.
3. Er hatte keine angemessene Kleidung und musste vor dem Regen Schutz suchen.

Seite 20

1. Er wurde aus dem Büro hinausgeworfen und ist jetzt arbeitslos.
2. Die neue Vorrichtung, die sie benutzten, erwies sich als sehr nützlich.
3. Trotz des Schmutzes und der Eile wurde die Operation erfolgreich ausgeführt.

Seite 22

1. Der Manager hatte die Absicht, mehr Personal zu beschäftigen, vorausgesetzt, dass Angebot und Nachfrage stabil *(stable)* blieben.
2. Sie war gezwungen, das Rauchen aufzugeben, um ihrem Kind eine sichere und gesunde Umgebung zu bieten *(give)*.
3. Die Prophezeiung, dass er sich das Genick brechen würde, wenn er sein Motorrad nicht sofort verkaufte, langweilte ihn nur.

Seite 24

1. Werkzeuge von minderer Qualität zu kaufen, zahlt sich auf die Dauer nicht aus.
2. Er wollte nur auf eine Minute vorbeischauen; nach zwei Stunden war er jedoch immer noch da.
3. Der Minister bekräftigte, dass das Wettrüsten um des Friedens willen beendet werden sollte.

Seite 26

1. Es ist wichtig, daß wir nach neuen Mitteln suchen, Schadstoffe zu vermeiden, besonders in der Landwirtschaft, so dass wir der Nachwelt das Land unbeschädigt hinterlassen *(leave for)*.
2. Es scheint, dass wir einen Überschuss an *(excess of)* Arbeitskräften und nicht genug Beschäftigung haben.
3. Wir müssen den Einwanderern das Leben erleichtern, die infolge von Rassendiskriminierung oft in echtem Elend leben.

Seite 28

1. Er beabsichtigte, Selbstmord zu begehen, weil sich seine Gesundheit verschlechterte.
2. Sie betrauerten den Tod des jungen Umweltschützers, und der Bürgermeister hielt *(make)* eine bewegende Rede.

3. Der Junge gehorchte seinem Vater und beendete seine Ausbildung, obwohl er von Beruf Landwirt werden wollte.

Seite 30

1. Der Koch schmolz die Butter und goss die Flüssigkeit in die Soße.
2. Er hatte einen Minderwertigkeitskomplex, weil er sich auffallend hässlich fand.
3. Das wirkliche Ziel seines Briefes war, sich an all den Leuten zu rächen, die mehr Erfolg gehabt hatten als er.

Seite 32

1. Die Hoffnung, viel Geld zu verdienen *(make)*, ist ein unverzichtbarer Anreiz in unserem Wirtschaftssystem.
2. Sparsame Autos können die nachteiligen Folgen für unsere Umwelt verringern.
3. Wegen seiner politischen Misserfolge war der Minister gezwungen zurückzutreten.

Seite 34

1. Sie bewarb sich bei *(to)* verschiedenen Firmen um eine Stelle und erkundigte sich nach den Beschäftigungsbedingungen.
2. Sie musste mit der Katastrophe alleine fertig werden, und daher wunderte ich mich nicht, dass ihre Gesichtszüge trauriger wurden.
3. Während des Semesters machte der Student bewusste Anstrengungen *(effort)*, sich Wissen anzueignen.

Seite 36

1. In der Regel gibt er sich Mühe, wirkungsvoll zu arbeiten, aber letzthin hat er viele seiner Termine *(appointment)* verschoben.
2. Die anderen Ärzte konnten sich den Schmerz nicht erklären, und ich verdanke es Dr. Jones, dass die entscheidende Diagnose *(diagnosis)* gestellt *(make)* wurde.
3. Denke an die Vor- und Nachteile des neuesten Modells, bevor du dich entscheidest, welches Auto für dich geeignet ist.

Seite 38

1. Mein alter Bekannter war ein ruhiger Mann, der in seinem Garten zu sitzen pflegte, wobei *(-ing)* er seine Pfeife rauchte und dieVögel beobachtete.
2. Die Gewerkschaft unterstützte die gewalttätigen Demonstrationen, als sich die Regierung weigerte *(refuse)*, den Arbeitern höhere Löhne anzubieten.
3. Es steht *(be)* außer Zweifel, dass er dafür bestraft werden wird, dass er das Haus besetzt hat.

Seite 40

1. Ohne Aufschub begannen sie damit, für die Kinder zu sorgen, die von ihren Eltern vernachlässigt worden waren.
2. Einige Leute glauben, dass sich die Beschäftigungsaussichten innerhalb der nächsten zehn Jahre allmählich verbessern werden.
3. Ich freue mich auf eine Zeit, da Probleme der Rassengleichheit überwunden sein werden *(present perfect)*.

Seite 42

1. Sie standen im Begriff, in ein geräumiges Haus zu ziehen, als er plötzlich seine Beschäftigung verlor.
2. Als Überraschung zum Geburtstag seiner Frau wählte der Professor einen Band über *(on)* Kunst aus.
3. Ich nehme *an,* dass der Patient kaum wusste, was ihn im Operationssaal erwartete.

Seite 44

1. Sie hatte keinen Erfolg bei *(fail in)* dem Versuch, den Streit um das Eigentum und die Bankkonten ihrer Eltern beizulegen.
2. Er war von *(with)* Neid auf seine Nachbarn erfüllt, die sowohl ein wertvolles Gemälde von Picasso als auch eine beeindruckende Sammlung alter Münzen besaßen.
3. Die Europäer, die den afrikanischen Kontinent erforschten, beraubten die Eingeborenen ihrer alten Lebensweise.

Seite 46

1. Obwohl seine Ersparnisse zu Ende gegangen waren, lehnte der Mann das Geldangebot ab, weil er nicht betteln wollte.
2. Die Hennen kratzten im Staub nach *(for)* Korn.
3. Der Präsident weigerte sich zurückzutreten, bevor er nicht *(until)* seine Pflicht getan und die Angelegenheit geregelt *(settle)* hatte.

Seite 48

1. Der afrikanische Athlet *(athlete)*, der während des Rennens kaum geschwitzt hatte, gewann den ersten Preis.
2. Trotz der Abwesenheit seiner strengen Großmutter war sein Benehmen ausgezeichnet, und er war zu allen höflich.
3. Seine feste Stimme und seine Freundlichkeit schienen mir vertraut und erinnerten mich an meinen Großvater.

Seite 50

1. Als der Gärtner den Zaun *(fence)* ausbesserte, entdeckte er zu seiner Freude eine Vielfalt von seltenen *(rare)* Blumen.
2. Der Händler erwähnte, dass er bald eine Reise ins Ausland machen würde.
3. Er trank selten Whisky, und selbst die winzige Flasche, die er als Geschenk erhalten hatte, machte ihn bald ziemlich fröhlich.

Seite 52

1. Johns männliche Eitelkeit und seine Neigung *(tendency)* zu prahlen enttäuschte seine Freunde, und sie begannen, ihn zu meiden.
2. Zu meiner großen Enttäuschung gaben sie uns nicht die Erlaubnis, unser Stück aufzuführen.
3. Alle Kinder begleiteten uns, und ich war froh, dass sie unser ganzes Gepäck zur Bushaltestelle trugen, wo wir den Fahrplan studierten.

Seite 54

1. Es gab einen Überschuss an Getreide, und der Bauer hatte folglich keinen Gewinn von seiner Ernte.
2. Das schüchterne Kind verbarg sein Gesicht, als die fremde Frau es berührte.
3. Der Chirurg *(surgeon)* machte einen Schnitt mit der Schere und *(-ing)* enthüllte dabei die Ursache der Krankheit.

Seite 56

1. Die Frau, die in der Bibliothek arbeitete, wurde wegen *(for)* ihrer fleißigen Art und ihrer Geduld bewundert
2. Ich schlage vor *(make + noun)*, dass du alle verfügbaren Zahlen sorgfältig studierst, bevor du die Situation beurteilst.
3. Es war offenkundig, dass er krank war und sichtbar leiden musste, denn er ergriff jede Gelegenheit, sich hinzusetzen und auszuruhen..

Seite 58

1. Ich muss gestehen, dass der Richter meiner Meinung nach voreingenommen gegen den Bürger war.
2. Aufeinanderfolgende Versuche, ein Treffen zustandezubringen, schlugen fehl, weil sie vergessen hatten, richtig dafür *(weglassen)* zu werben.
3. Er erkannte die Entschlossenheit seines Freundes und bemühte sich, ihn dem Professor vorzustellen.

Seite 60

1. Sie versprachen, dass er seinen Anteil an der Belohnung im Voraus bekommen würde.
2. Die endgültige Beurteilung hängt vom Erfolg des Lehrlings in seiner Pflichtprüfung ab.
3. Der Manager behauptete, dass er nicht einmal eine einzige Aktie besäße.

Seite 62

1. Ich war mir bewusst, dass meine Freunde wohlhabend sind; trotzdem glaubte ich nicht, dass sie so viel kostbares Geld verschwenden würden.
2. Es gibt Beweise *(Singular)*, dass er in der Prüfung betrog, um seine Note zu verbessern.
3. Um die wachsende Nachfrage zu befriedigen, dehnten sie ihr Geschäft aus.

Seite 64

1. Nach seiner Krankheit sah er ziemlich mager und gebrechlich aus und fiel oft in Ohnmacht.
2. Man *(Passiv)* gab ihm die Schuld für das Misslingen ihrer Pläne, und alle, außer den treuesten seiner Freunde, ließen ihn im Stich.
3. Die Leute bemitleideten ihn, auch wenn er sein Urteil tapfer aufnahm.

Seite 66

1. Er beklagte sich, dass sie ihn nach dem Aufruhr daran gehindert hatten, die Vorlesungen *(lectures)* seines *(in)* Faches zu besuchen.
2. Sie zögerten nicht, die Grenze zu überqueren, die die beiden Länder trennte.
3. Sie war erleichtert, als *(Infinitiv)* sie hörte, dass genügend Zeit sein würde, ein Treffen einzurichten.

Seite 68

1. Sie hatte das Bügeleisen in einer Schaufensterauslage gesehen und freute sich sehr über den Kauf.
2. Die Saison begann im Juni mit der Ankunft der ersten Touristen, die gekommen waren, um die Sehenswürdigkeiten zu besichtigen *(see)*.
3. Er war sehr erfinderisch, und als er mit dem Inspektor telefonierte, verstellte er seine Stimme, um ihn zu verwirren.

Seite 70

1. Er war überzeugt, dass es genügend Quellenmaterial gab, um die Ansiedlung bis zu den Römern zurückzuverfolgen.
2. Das Kapital, das erforderlich war, um den durchschnittlichen Gewinn der Firma aufrechtzuerhalten, belief sich auf zehntausend Pfund.
3. Zu seiner Erleichterung konnten die seltsamen Herzbeschwerden *(Sing.)*, die ihn beunruhigt *(=gestört)* hatten, sofort behandelt werden.

Seite 72

1. Der Student musste seine ganze Fertigkeit und seine Phantasie einsetzen *(use)*, um die Eintrittsanforderungen zu erfüllen.
2. Er hatte zum Krieg in der Wüste dadurch beigetragen, dass *(by)* er die notwendigen Waffen lieferte.
3. Sie war von der Vorliebe der Italiener für blonde Frauen erstaunt.

Seite 74

1. Er war daran gewöhnt, eine Menge Freizeit zu haben und jeden Monat einen großen Geldbetrag zu erhalten.
2. Die laufenden Ausgaben für den Gütertransport erwiesen sich als zu hoch.
3. Die Schwierigkeit war, dass er das Auto nicht zu einem vernünftigen Preis verkaufen konnte, ohne den Kunden zu täuschen.

Seite 76

1. Blumensträuße und Reklame wurden unter der Menge verteilt.
2. Wie kannst du es wagen, einen so großzügigen Mann mit solchem Stolz zu behandeln?
3. Nachdem die Entscheidung gefallen *(make + Passiv)* war, wurden von der schuldigen Partei die Gerichtskosten gefordert.

Seite 78

1. Er hatte seine Tochter gerne und war besorgt um ihre Behandlung im Krankenhaus.
2. Sie leisteten *(offer)* dem Feind nur geringen Widerstand.
3. Der neue Richter wurde wegen *(for)* seiner Erfahrung mit *(of)* solchen Prozessen ernannt.

Seite 80

1. Wegen seines Berufes als Privatdetektiv wurde vorgeschlagen, dass er die Angelegenheit untersuchen sollte.
2. Das alte Rohr war beschädigt worden, und das Wasser floss in den Erdboden.
3. Nachdem er den Draht vorsichtig an der Batterie befestigt hatte, gab es eine fürchterliche *(terrible)* Explosion.

Seite 82

1. Nach den unvermeidlichen Anfangsschwierigkeiten begann das Unternehmen glatt zu laufen, und wir konnten mit anderen Firmen konkurrieren.
2. Nachdem er in einen Autounfall verwickelt war, erhielt Mr. MacDonald ein künstliches Bein, aber er stellte sich bald darauf ein.
3. Ich verzweifele oft an der offensichtlichen Gleichgültigkeit mancher Leute gegenüber der Armut.

WORD FAMILIES

Complete the following word families using your "Arbeitswortschatz" and, if necessary, a good dictionary for the forms marked with an asterisk (*). Make sure you know the meaning of all entries.

	NOUN	ADJECTIVE	VERB
1	prosperity	prosperous	
2			urge
3	satisfaction		
4	success		
5	*	*	collect
6			tempt
7	regret	*	
8		considerable	
9		annoying	
10			persuade
11	admiration	*	
12			unite
13	grade	*	
14		*	decide
15		remarkable	
16	*	*	separate
17	volunteer		
18			operate
19	benefit	*	*
20	*		communicate
21		original	*

	NOUN	ADJECTIVE	VERB
22		harmful	
23			offend
24	*	comprehensive	
25	suspicion	*	
26		economical	
27	strength		*
28		violent	*
29	impression		
30			value
31	length		*
32			bias
33	justice		
34			introduce
35	advice	*	
36	irritation		
37		*	contradict
38		confused	
39	*		invent
40		comparative	
41			delight
42	competition	*	

OPPOSITES

Make the following words mean the opposite by adding one of these prefixes

dis- il- im- in- mis- un-

1	sufficient
2	appear
3	movable
4	employed
5	comfort
6	legal
7	avoidable
8	visible
9	calculable
10	patient
11	believe
12	conscious
13	approve
14	capable
15	familiar
16	considerate
17	used
18	polite

19	accustomed
20	dependent
21	common
22	engage
23	difference
24	comparable
25	fortune
26	offensive
27	rest
28	justice
29	calculate
30	fair
31	developed
32	content
33	kind
34	experienced
35	connect
36	like

37	efficient
38	biased
39	ability
40	behave
41	adequate
42	able
43	safe
44	voluntary
45	pleasant
46	human
47	obedient
48	measurable
49	skilled
50	handle
51	equality
52	trust
53	agree
54	liberal

PUZZLES	**PUZZLES**	*PUZZLES*	PUZZLES
PUZZLES	*PUZZLES*	PUZZLES	**PUZZLES**
PUZZLES	PUZZLES	**PUZZLES**	*PUZZLES*
PUZZLES	**PUZZLES**	*PUZZLES*	PUZZLES
PUZZLES	*PUZZLES*	PUZZLES	**PUZZLES**
💣*ZZLES*	PUZZLES	**PUZZLES**	*PUZZLES*
PUZZLES	**PUZZLES**	*PUZZLES*	PUZZLES
PUZZLES	*PUZZLES*	PUZZLES	**PUZZLES**
PUZZLES	PUZZLES	**PUZZLES**	*PUZZLES*
PUZZLES	**PUZZLES**	*PUZZLES*	PUZZLES
PUZZLES	*PUZZLES*	PUZZLES	**PUZZLES**
PUZZLES	PUZZLES	**PUZZLES**	*PUZZLES*
PUZZLES	**PUZZLES**	*PUZZLES*	PUZZLES
PUZZLES	*PUZZLES*	PUZZLES	**PUZZLES**
PUZZLES	PUZZLES	**PUZZLES**	*PUZZLES*
PUZZLES	**PUZZLES**	*PUZZLES*	PUZZLES
PUZZLES	*PUZZLES*	PUZZLES	**PUZZ** ☞

CROSSWORD PUZZLE

Please repeat the "Arbeitswortschatz" from page 4 to 12 before going to work on this puzzle. The letters in circles - read in the given order - name an animal that can become 400 years old.

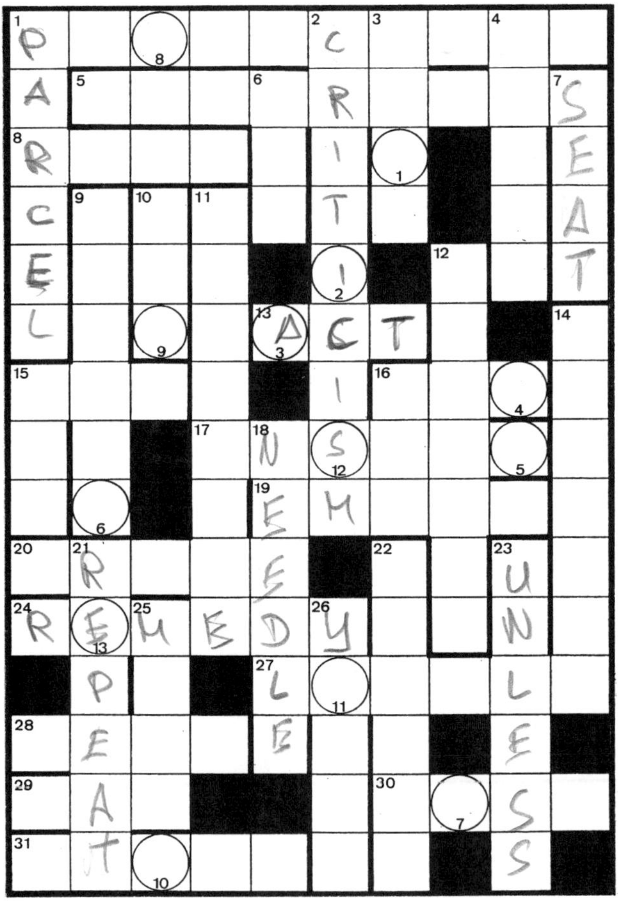

ACROSS

A **▷1** is a detail * You may **▷5** someone by telling him the frank but unpleasant truth * not thanking for a favour is **▷8** behaviour * an **▷13** can be a law * you **▷15** a boat if you move it by armpower * a can is also called **▷16** * you **▷17** if you are not content with something other than you want * **▷19** is the opposite of full * some students **▷20** that teachers are sadists * a **▷24** will put an end to trouble or illness * astronauts are not **▷27** to find life on the planet Mars * instead of buying a house you can also **▷28** one * the opposite of happy is **▷29** * the parents' death is a great **▷30** to their children * warehouses often have a big and valuable **▷31** of goods

DOWN

A **▷1** is a packet * a discussion of a theatre performance or a book is a **▷2** * to **▷3** someone means to ask him passionately * **▷4** means 'up to now' (2 words) * an **▷6** can be a weapon * you sit on a **▷7** * you write down information in a **▷9** * **▷10** can mean 'but' * 'go on' is the same as **▷11** * some people can **▷12** with two fingers in their mouths * an **▷14** is an investigation * meat which is neither fried nor cooked is **▷15** * a **▷16** can be some extra money for the waiter * you need a **▷18** and thread to fix a loose button of your shirt * If you **▷21** something you do it again * you are **▷22** to remember this word because it has already been asked in this puzzle * **▷23** means 'if not' * if you **▷25** something you take care of it * to **▷26** can mean to give in

1	2	3	4	5	6	7	8	9	10	11	12	13

LETTER BOARD

Please repeat page 14 to 24 of your "Arbeitswortschatz" carefully before you start working on this letter board. It hides 24 terms to be found either in one line horizontally, vertically or diagonally from left to right downwards. Then read the remaining letters line by line and you will find an English proverb that also applies to the learning of English words. Good luck!

P	O	P	U	L	A	T	I	O	N	I	G	F	A	F
E	A	B	T	W	R	A	P	F	H	E	A	S	E	I
R	I	C	T	N	G	S	M	F	I	S	D	W	O	L
S	K	R	E	R	T	T	N	E	C	K	G	K	H	T
U	I	I	S	S	U	E	D	N	S	P	E	E	C	H
A	N	O	T	E	O	S	I	C	N	S	T	Y	G	S
S	D	I	I	E	Q	U	I	E	T	T	A	I	S	T
I	W	O	T	D	R	M	O	V	E	T	H	G	D	U
V	O	I	G	E	N	U	I	N	E	N	G	W	E	F
E	N	V	I	R	O	N	M	E	N	T	E	L	L	F

the number of people in a country is called p-- * the things around us is our e-- * if you do something with e-- it is not difficult * when people come together to form a group they u-- * a synonym of 'friendly' is k-- * you must be p-- to convince others * a tin-opener for example is a useful g-- * if you m-- you don't stand still * people who want to sell things at your front door and won't go away are obtru-- *(a little help from the author:* -sive*)* * when you make something extremely full, for example a suitcase, you s-- it * if you dress elegantly and make a good impression you show your good t-- * when you talk to a large audience you make a s-- * 'speed' can be a synonym of p-- * if you publish a newspaper you i-- it * if you break your n-- you'll be dead * crossing the road at red light is an o-- * a n-- is a short message in written form * a synonym of 'calm' is q-- * to have a harvest you must sow s-- * g-- means almost the same as 'real' * instead of 'dirt' you can also say f-- * a piece of information is a m-- * you need a k-- to open a locked door * you w-- a parcel with a piece of paper * a k-- is part of a piano

SOLUTION

....

....

SYLLABLES

Please repeat your 'Arbeitswortschatz' first, then try to find 20 words connected from the list below. No syllable must be left. The first letters of the words you found tell you about the biggest library in the world, which holds about six million books in a museum (All words can be found between pages 24 and 36)

1	11 ....
2.	12. ....
3	13 ....
4	14 ....
5	15 ....
6	16 ....
7	17 ....
8	18 ....
9	19 ....
10.	20 ....

able - al - ard - belt - cen - cite - dis - em - er - eral - ery - ex - face - feri - haz

hole - in - in - in - ing - ing - is - le - ly - man - ment - mis - or- pens - per

ploy - pow - re - sev - strik - sue - sur - tack - tem - tire - tive - train - ug - usu

1. air is it for human living 2. when you are happy you are in a good one 3. you do it when you publish a magazine 4. it means the same as 'some different' 5. you do it when you start on a problem 6. you have it in your sock when your toe sticks out 7. you do it if you rouse up someone's feelings 8. one needs it to fasten one's trousers 9. you do it when you get your old age pension 10. it is a motivation 11. it is what you have learnt in order to do your job 12. being worth less than others 13. the outside of something, e.g. the sea 14. danger, risk 15. the number of people working, e.g. in a factory, are called so 16. the opposite of 'beautiful' 17. it can mean 'impressing' 18. people without a job are looking for it 19. it is as it always is 20. many people of the Third World live in this condition

SPEEDY SNAIL

You should know the words from page 36 to 44 before solving Speedy Snail's puzzle. The last letter of each term is the first of the following. Sit back and relax - but don't work at a snail's pace!

when you say "I won't do my homework now, but later" you ... your work * committing a crime is an ... thing * only the ... news is interesting * if you want to go for a swim in the sea you should be careful of the ... * the ... of your car to a friend can mean the beginning of great trouble * the aim of Scott was to ... the polar region * the learning of English words is only ... if you don't forget to repeat them regularly * the ... of making a career can make people work hard * seeing a performance in a good ... can be a great pleasure * it is a good idea to .... a partner thoroughly before marrying him or her * only an ... plan can be a really good one * emancipated women demand the ... of the sexes

ODD MAN OUT

Please repeat the words from page 46 to 52 first. Each of the following groups of terms contains one word which has no association or common idea together with the other three. Find out this 'odd man' and mark the letter of the word the number of which is in the right column of each block. Then insert all eleven letters one after the other into the unfinished sentence and you will know of what material George Washington's third teeth were.

1	savings dust loan price	4
2	prize merchant beggar female	5
3	attack knock cut down refuse	2
4	boast disappoint increase threaten	4
5	joint except connection attached	1
6	growth avoid decline advance	1
7	discover lack humble beg	1
8	merry kindness joy gift	3
9	abroad schedule behaviour journey	7
10	remember swallow doubt believe	6
11	advance accompany glad resign	4

1	H	2	Y		W	3	4	5		M	6	7	E		O	8		W	9	10	11

LETTERS & NUMBERS

Here you can check your knowledge of the words from page 54 to 62. Each letter corresponds to a number, which will help you to get along. If you read the letters corresponding to

20 19 4 4 6 7 16 10 1 21 6 12

you will learn what could be seen in the sky both on Mark Twain's birthday and the day he died.

1. honour gained by achievements **2 4 1 5 7**	8. rather valuable **15 5 6 10 13 1 11 16**
2. way in which a thing happens **21 19 8 8 6 5**	9. form an opinion about **9 11 3 2 6**
3. learner of a trade **19 15 15 5 5 8 12 13 10 6**	10. hard-working **3 13 4 13 2 6 8 12**
4. that which produces an effect **10 19 11 16 6**	11. get into contact with **12 1 11 10 20**
5. suitable, handy **10 1 8 18 6 8 13 6 8 12**	12. person living in a town **10 13 12 13 14 6 8**
6. synonym of profit **2 19 13 8**	13. start **4 19 11 8 10 20**
7. number of things lying one upon the other **15 13 4 6**	14. change from one form into another **10 1 8 18 6 5 12**

THE TRAGIC CONFESSION

Reading the following text you will find that a number of words have been left out. To help you fill in those thirteen blanks there is a list of fifteen words at the end of the story. Which of them fit where into the text? All words are taken from the 'Arbeitswortschatz' pages 64 to 72.

"You're under arrest" said the police inspector and took a pair of hand-cuffs out of his pocket. "Come on now!" Gary Fabriciano had lost the game, and he knew he was the victim of Rod Marley's revenge.

In their childhood Rod and Gary had been the closest friends you could possibly 1 .... They had 2 .... the same class and had been together almost every day in their hometown of Hastings. One day, however, it 3 .... to Gary to steal Rod's

beautiful red scooter - nobody knows exactly why - and threw it into a pond near their favourite play-ground. Rod was filled with hatred and whispered "One day I'll take revenge on you". Yet he never again 4 .... about the incident.

At the age of 19 Fabriciano left his home town for New York to find some work there, or to make his fortune with his Italian relations who seemed to be involved in some obscure business. On the day of his departure the two friends 5 .... the plan that they would meet again at the "Golden Eagle" - a pub in which they had often had a pint of beer together - exactly twenty years later, no matter how far each of them had to travel. ---

"Gary?" asked Rod 6 .... , as a 7 .... , well-dressed man of about 40 years entered the "Golden Eagle". "Good heavens, my old chap Rod", shouted Gary enthusiastically, "how've you been all these years?" Fabriciano had obviously made a lot of money in the States, which could be guessed from his big diamond rings and a valuable golden watch, together with his expensive outfit. He seemed to be proud of his achievements and soon began to outline his story. "You're my 8 .... friend. Rod, so you'll be the only one in the world to hear my story truly. I've 9 .... a great lot of money with my gang and the police have never succeeded in catching me. Above all, they suspect murder, but they don't have 10 .... proof that it was me who killed the two clerks in our latest bank robbery two weeks ago."

Suddenly Gary stopped in 11 .... , while his face was expressing pure 12 .... "Hey, you're not Rod", he cried, "twenty years is a very long time, but not long enough to change a face so much". "You're right, Fabriciano", said the police inspector calmly. "Mr. Marley gave us a tip, I was filled with 13 .... , and so I'm here today instead of him. I must admit that we don't look much alike. You're under arrest".

--- An old rusty scooter still lay in the mud on the ground of a pond in Hastings / Sussex.

...	confusion
...	complained
...	relieve
...	lean
...	hesitatingly

...	sufficient
...	faithful
...	curiosity
...	fright
...	comfort

...	attended
...	conceived
...	imagine
...	piled up
...	occured

NETWORK

words from page 74 to page 82 - Which is the only town in the USA with a Royal Palace? The encircled letters will help you to find the answer.

ACROSS

2 information about a product (e.g. in a newspaper)

4 without fear

5 cost

8 act towards, behave to

10 have the courage to do something

11 make ready

12 thing wrongly done

14 not more than

15 excellent, magnificent

16 large-scale exhibition

17 say that something is not true

19 having common sense

21 single unit or point (in a list)

22 coming at the end

24 unfilled space

29 mislead on purpose

31 generally accepted behaviour

32 hate extremely

33 settlement of a question

DOWN

1 under, below

2 quantity, sum

3 believe that something will happen

6 process of showing by words

7 make a positive development

9 give, offer

11 thing done to get ready

13 task, enterprise

16 fix firmly

18 moreover

20 see, notice

23 occupation

25 show to be true without doubt

26 enlarge, make longer

27 achievement not reached before

28 place with walls or buildings around it

30 rooms on one floor as residence

1	2	3	4	5	6	7	8

CROSSWORD FOR EXPERTS

All terms contained in this puzzle are taken from your "Arbeitswortschatz". So if you have learnt thoroughly you should succeed. The letters in circles form a word that expresses the authors' respect for your achievements.

ACROSS **1** surveys of public attitudes (two words) **10** feeling at a surprising situation **12** rough plan showing the shape of sth. **14** get away from **16** behave towards **18** opposite of 'female' **19** what you must do **22** group of persons joined together **24** person employed for work in a household **25** sth. you sit on **27** doing no work, not active **29** being busy **31** settlement of a problem **34** full of strong desire **35** taking place every year **37** become liquid through heating **40** prevent s.o. from entering (two words) **44** synonym of 'already' **46** opposite of 'wide' **47** clean by rubbing **48** pay no attention to **50** fame won by great deeds **52** get rid of; deal with **56** happy, cheerful **58** common **60** preparation for war **62** unfilled space **63** up to the time when **65** soft or easily hurt **66** pointing (e.g. a gun) towards **67** not relying on others **68** examine thoroughly **69** get pleasure from

DOWN **1** be in debt to **2** synonym of 'own' **3** become greater or more **4** otherwise (two words) **5** pay attention to **6** unmixed, clean **7** say sth. that you know is not true **8** opposite of 'dry' **9** additional part, enlargement **11** harm or injury **13** person associated with a place by birth **15** corridor in a building **16** examination in a law court **17** sth. needed **20** synonym of 'say' **21** teenager **23** starting point **26** deal with, attack (a problem) **28** avoidance of waste, of energy, or money **30** opposite of 'beautiful' **31** become worse **32** not to fail **33** small apparatus **36** having a horizontal surface **38** make sth. seem bigger, better etc. **39** synonym of 'halt' **41** belief **42** instrument for opening a locked door **43** try to persuade, press on s.b. **45** statement of received or paid money **49** think of sth. as possible **51** give a result or profit **53** self-murder **54** protected from **55** choose by vote **57** supply of sth. kept for later use **59** loss of self-respect through dishonourable behaviour **61** take care of **64** position in a scale **65** piece of advice

1	2	3	4	5	6	7	8	9	10	11	12	13	14	15

SOLUTION / SENTENCES

Page 4

1. He was embarrassed when I insisted on reading the criticism of his new book. 2. In/over/ the last few years he has developed the bad habit of being rude to his friends. 3. They urged him in vain to sell them his prosperous firm.

Page 6

1. The two sides negotiated to improve the situation and to bring the misuse of arms to a conclusion. 2. The police continued their inquiry into the sad fate of the youth. 3. The /pupil/student/ read the passage briefly and then inquired about some words.

Page 8

1. The hostile powers spent more time arguing than trying to handle the urgent problem of disarmament. 2. Despite the cold he enjoyed sitting on the bench in his garden. 3. My grandmother tries to guard against the loss of her money by keeping it in an empty tin.

Page 10

1. The official who had robbed the bank was found guilty and dismissed. 2. After a thorough examination the doctor repeated his advice twice and prescribed a remedy for the stomach /pains/ache. 3. On the whole, the result of the election seemed to satisfy them.

Page 12

1. She reported that in one of the suburbs a new subway was being built. 2. In accordance with the new act every civil servant had to make a report about the particulars of his /work/job. 3. It was the servants' /job/task/ to collect the rent and the tips.

Page 14

1. I particularly regret to announce that the annual profit has fallen considerably. 2. I wished the handsome young man happiness, luck and great achievements in his work. 3. Meanwhile/meantime/ they had set up the tent while I was sitting on a cushion buried in thoughts.

Page 16

1. I was full of admiration when I heard that the union leader had had the courage to take the necessary /steps/measures. 2. Please take off that shirt with the filthy collar. 3. I couldn't persuade him to stop smoking.

Page 18

1. The thieves opened the door with the stolen key and stuffed their bags with all kinds of things. 2. The owner blamed the customer for the damage and he was requested to leave the shop. 3. He had no adequate clothing and had to take shelter from the rain.

Page 20

1. He was turned out of the office and is now unemployed. 2. The new gadget which they employed turned out to be very useful. 3. In spite of/despite/ the filth and the rush the operation was accomplished successfully.

Page 22

1. The manager had the intention of employing more staff provided that the supply and demand remained stable. 2. She was compelled to give up smoking in order to give her /baby/child/ a safe and healthy environment. 3. The prediction that he would break his neck if he didn't sell his motor-bike at once merely bored him.

Page 24

1. Buying tools of inferior quality doesn't pay in the long run. 2. He only wanted to drop in for a minute; after two hours, however, he was still there. 3. The minister confirmed that the arms race should be stopped for the sake of peace.

Page 26

1. It is important that we search for new means of avoiding pollutants, especially in agriculture, so that we leave the land undamaged for posterity. 2. It seems that we have an excess of manpower and not enough employment. 3. We must ease the lives of the immigrants, who, due to racial discrimination, often live in pure misery.

Page 28

1. He intended to commit suicide because his health was deteriorating. 2. They mourned the death of the young environmentalist, and the mayor made a moving speech. 3. The boy obeyed his father and finished his training, although he wanted to become a farmer by vocation.

Page 30

1. The cook melted the butter and poured the liquid into the sauce. 2. He had an inferiority complex because he found himself strikingly ugly. 3. The actual object of his letter was to retaliate on all those people who had had more success than he.

Page 32

1. The hope of making much money is an indispensable incentive in our economy. 2. Economical cars can reduce the detrimental effects on our environment. 3. Due to his political failures the minister was forced to /retire/resign.

Page 34

1. She applied to several firms and inquired about the terms of employment. 2. She had to cope with the disaster alone and therefore I did not wonder that her features grew sadder. 3. During the term the student made conscious efforts to acquire knowledge.

Page 36

1. As a rule he takes pains to work efficiently but of late he has postponed many of his appointments. 2. The other doctors could not account for the pain and I owe it to Dr. Jones that the crucial diagnosis was made. 3. Keep the advantages and disadvantages of the latest model in mind before /deciding/you decide/ which car is suitable for you.

Page 38

1. My old acquaintance was a calm man who used to sit in his garden, smoking his pipe and observing the birds. 2. The trade union supported the violent demonstrations when the government refused to offer the workers higher wages. 2. It is beyond doubt that he will be punished for occupying the house.

Page 40

1. Without delay they began to look after the children who had been neglected by their parents. 2. Some people fancy that employment prospects will improve gradually within the next /decade/ten years. 3. I look forward to a time when problems of racial equality have been overcome.

Page 42

1. They were about to move into a spacious house when suddenly he lost his occupation. 2. As a surprise for his wife's birthday the professor selected a volume on art. 3. I suppose (that) the patient scarcely knew what was /awaiting/ waiting for/ him in the (operation) theatre.

Page 44

1. She failed in her attempt to settle the quarrel about her parents' property and bank accounts. 2. He was filled with jealousy of his neighbours who /owned/ possessed/ both a valuable painting by Picasso and an impressing collection of old coins. 3. The Europeans who explored the African continent deprived the natives of their old way of life.

Page 46

1. Although his savings had run out, the man declined the offer of money because he did not want to beg. 2. The hens scratched in the dust for grain. 3. The president refused to resign until he had done his duty and settled the matter.

Page 48

1. The African athlete, who had hardly sweated during the race, won (the) first prize. 2. In spite of/despite/ the absence of his severe grandmother his behaviour was excellent and he was polite to everyone. 3. His firm voice and his kindness seemed familiar to me and reminded me of my grandfather.

Page 50

1. When the gardener mended the fence he discovered to his joy a variety of rare flowers. 2. The merchant mentioned that he would soon /make/be making/ a journey abroad. 3. He seldom drank whisky, and even the tiny bottle (which) he had received as a gift soon made him rather merry.

Page 52

1. John's male vanity and his tendency to boast disappointed his friends and they began to avoid him. 2. To my great disappointment they did not give us permission to /perform/stage/ our play. 3. All the children accompanied us, and I was glad that they carried all our luggage to the bus-stop, where we studied the schedule.

Page 54

1. There was a surplus of grain and the farmer consequently did not gain from his harvest. 2. The shy child hid its face when the strange woman touched it. 3. The surgeon made a cut with the scissors, revealing the cause of the disease.

Page 56

1. The woman who worked in the library was admired for her diligent manners and her patience. 2. I make the proposal that you study all /available figures/figures available/ carefully before judging the situation. 3. It was evident that he was ill and had to suffer visibly, because he was taking every opportunity to sit down and (have a) rest.

Page 58

1. I must confess that in my opinion the judge was biased against the citizen. 2. Successive attempts to bring about a meeting failed because they had forgotten to advertise properly. 3. He recognised his friend's determination and made an effort to introduce him to the professor.

Page 60

1. They promised that he would /get/receive/ his share of the reward in advance. 2. The final judgement depends on the apprentice's success in his compulsory exam. 3. The manager claimed that he did not even possess a single share.

Page 62

1. I was aware that my friends are affluent; even so I didn't think they would waste so much precious money. 2. There is proof that he cheated in the exam to improve his mark. 3. To meet the growing demand they expanded their business.

Page 64
1. After his illness he looked rather lean and fragile and often fainted. 2. He was given the blame for the failure of their plans, and all but the most faithful of his friends deserted him. 3. The people pitied him, even though he took his sentence bravely.
Page 66
1. He complained that, after the riot, they had prevented him from attending the lectures of his subject. 2. They didn't hesitate to cross the border that separated the two countries. 3. She was relieved to hear that there would be sufficient time to arrange a meeting.
Page 68
1. She had seen the iron in a window display and was very pleased with the bargain. 2. The season began in June with the arrival of the first tourists who had come to see the sights. 3. He was very inventive, and when he phoned the inspector, he disguised his voice to confuse him.
Page 70
1. He was convinced that there was enough source material to trace back the settlement to the Romans. 2. The capital required to maintain the firm's average profit amounted to ten thousand pounds. 3. To his relief the curious heart complaint which had disturbed him could immediately be treated.
Page 72
1. The student had to use all his skill and imagination in order to /meet/fulfill the entrance requirements. 2. He had contributed to the war in the desert by /delivering/supplying/ the necessary weapons. 3. She was astonished by the Italians' preference for fair women.
Page 74
1. He was accustomed to having a lot of spare time and to receiving a large amount of money every month. 2. The current expenses for the carriage of goods proved to be too high. 3. The trouble was that he couldn't sell the car at a reasonable price without deceiving the customer.
Page 76
1. Bunches of flowers and advertisements were distributed among the crowd. 2. How do you dare to/how dare you/ treat such a generous man with such pride? 3. After the decision had been made the guilty party was charged the court expenses.
Page 78
1. He was fond of his daughter and anxious about her treatment in the hospital. 2. They offered only slight resistance to the enemy. 3. The new judge was appointed for his experience of such trials.
Page 80
1. On account of his profession as private detective it was proposed that he should investigate the matter. 2. The ancient pipe had been damaged and the water flowed into the soil. 3. After he had cautiously fastened the wire to the battery there was a terrible blast.
Page 82
1. After the inevitable initial difficulties the enterprise began to run smoothly and we could compete with other firms. 2, After he had been/being/ involved in a car /accident/crash/ Mr. MacDonald received an artificial leg, but he soon adapted to it. 3. I often despair of some people's obvious indifference towards poverty.

SOLUTION WORD EXERCISES

WORD FAMILIES

1. prosperity/prosper 2. urgency/urgent 3. satisfactory/satisfy 4. successful/succeed 5. collection/collective 6. temptation/ tempting 7. regrettable/regret 8. consideration/consider 9. annoyance/annoy 10. persuasion/persuasive 11. admirable/admire 12. union/united 13. gradual/grade 14. decision/decisive 15. remark/remark 16. separation/separable 17. voluntary/volunteer 18. operation/operative 19. beneficial/benefit 20. communication/communicative 21. original/originate 22. harm/harm 23. offence/offensive 24. comprehension/comprehend 25. suspicious/ suspect 26. economy/economize 27. strong/strengthen 28. violence/violate 29. impressive/impress 30. value/valuable 31. long/lengthen 32.bias/biased 33. just/justify 34. introduction/introductory 35. advisable/advise 36. irritable/irritate 37. contradiction/contradictory 38. confusion/confuse 39. invention/inventive 40. comparison/compare 41. delight/delightful 42. competitive/compete

OPPOSITES

1. insufficient 2. disappear 3. immovable 4. unemployed 5. discomfort 6. illegal 7. unavoidable 8. invisible 9. incalculable 10. impatient 11. disbelieve 12. unconscious 13. disapprove 14. incapable 15. unfamiliar 16. inconsiderate 17. unused 18. impolite 19. unaccustomed 20. independent 21. uncommon 22. disengage 23. indifference 24. incomparable 25. misfortune 26. inoffensive 27. unrest 28. injustice 29. miscalculate 30. unfair 31. undeveloped 32. discontent 33. unkind 34. inexperienced 35. disconnect 36. unlike 37. inefficient 38. unbiased 39. inability 40. misbehave 41. inadequate 42. unable 43. unsafe 44. involuntary 45. unpleasant 46. inhuman 47. disobedient 48. immeasurable 49. unskilled 50. mishandle 51. inequality 52. mistrust 53. disagree 54. illiberal

SOLUTION / PUZZLES

CROSSWORD PUZZLE

ACROSS 1 particular 5 embarrass 8 rude 13 act 15 row 16 tin 17 insist 19 empty 20 argue 24 remedy 27 likely 28 rent 29 sad 30 loss 31 stock

DOWN 1 parcel 2 criticism 3 urge 4 as yet 6 arm 7 seat 9 report 10 yet 11 continue 12 whistle 14 inquiry 15 raw 16 tip 18 needle 21 repeat 22 likely 23 unless 25 mind 26 yield GIANT TORTOISE

LETTERBOARD

P	O	P	U	L	A	T	I	O	N	I	G	F	A	F
E	A	B	T	W	R	A	P	F	H	E	A	S	E	I
R	I	C	T	N	G	S	M	F	I	S	D	W	O	L
S	K	R	E	R	T	T	N	E	C	K	G	K	H	T
U	I	I	S	S	U	E	D	N	S	P	E	E	C	H
A	N	O	T	E	O	S	I	C	N	S	T	Y	G	S
S	D	I	I	E	Q	U	I	E	T	T	A	I	S	T
I	W	O	T	D	R	M	O	V	E	T	H	G	D	U
V	O	I	G	E	N	U	I	N	E	N	G	W	E	F
E	N	V	I	R	O	N	M	E	N	T	E	L	L	F

IF A THING IS WORTH DOING IT IS WORTH DOING WELL

SYLLABLES

1 indispensable 2 temper 3 issue 4 several 5 tackle 6 hole 7 excite 8 belt 9 retire 10 incentive 11 training 12 inferior 13 surface 14 hazard 15 manpower 16 ugly 17 striking 18 employment 19 usual 20 misery
IT IS THE BRITISH MUSEUM

SPEEDY SNAIL

postpone - evil - latest - tides - sale explore efficient - thought - theatre examine elaborate - equality

ODD MAN OUT

(Connecting idea in brackets) 1 dust (money) 2 prize (person) 3 refuse (physical work) 4 increase (unpleasant activity) 5 except (connection) 6 avoid (development) 7 discover (poorness) 8 gift (pleasant feeling) 9 behaviour (travel) 10 swallow (think) 11 glad (move)
THEY WERE MADE OF WOOD

LETTERS & NUMBERS

1 glory 2 manner 3 apprentice 4 cause 5 convenient 6 gain 7 pile 8 precious 9 judge 10 diligent 11 touch 12 citizen 13 launch 14 convert HALLEYS COMET

THE TRAGIC CONFESSION

1 imagine 2 attended 3 occurred 4 complained 5 conceived 6 hesitatingly 7 lean 8 faithful 9 piled up 10 sufficient 11 confusion 12 fright 13 curiosity

NETWORK

ACROSS 2 advertisement 4 bold 5 expense 8 treat 10 dare 11 prepare 12 fault 14 mere 15 splendid 16 fair 17 deny 19 reasonable 21 item 22 final 24 gap 29 deceive 31 custom 32 detest 33 decision DOWN 1 beneath 2 amount 3 expect 6 expression 7 progress 9 present 11 preparation 13 undertaking 16 fasten 18 besides 20 remark 23 profession 25 prove 26 extend 27 record 28 court 30 flat
HONOLULU

CROSSWORD FOR EXPERTS

ACROSS 1 opinion polls 10 wonder 12 outline 14 escape 16 treat 18 male 19 duty 22 association 24 servant 25 seat 27 idle 29 engaged 31 decision 34 eager 35 annual 37 melt 40 lock out 44 yet 46 narrow 47 wipe 48 neglect 50 glory 52 dispose 56 merry 58 usual 60 armament 62 gap 63 till 65 tender 66 aim 67 independent 68 explore 69 enjoy

DOWN 1 owe 2 possess 3 increase 4 or else 5 note 6 pure 7 lie 8 wet 9 extension 11 damage 13 native 15 passage 16 trial 17 requirement 20 utter 21 youth 23 origin 26 tackle 28 economy 30 ugly 31 deteriorate 32 succeed 33 gadget 36 level 38 exaggerate 39 stop 41 opinion 42 key 43 urge 45 account 49 imagine 51 yield 53 suicide 54 safe 55 elect 57 store 59 shame 61 mind 64 rank 65 tip CONGRATULATIONS